A Field Guide to the
CRYPTIDS
of North America

Dr. Courtney A. Shepherd

The Howecycle Press
Minneapolis

A Field Guide to the Cryptids of North America

The Howecycle Press
Minneapolis, Minnesota

ISBN 978-1540444257

For Rose Marie,
stay curious.

Table of Contents

Introduction

The perception among the general populace is that cryptozoology is a field full of kooks, crackpots, and delusionals. Who in their right mind, the skeptic asks, would spend their precious and limited time searching for animals that do not exist? And most people take it as a matter of faith that cryptids are, in fact, mythical creatures. But we, dear readers, know better. The list of cryptids that have been discovered, documented, and cataloged is extensive. Why, then, does cryptozoology remain ignored in a dank and shadowy corner of the Hall of Science? What is keeping it from basking in the light of public acceptance?

The simple answer is that once a cryptid is discovered it moves from the realm of cryptozoology into the realm of biology. What chance for respect does a field have if its most glorious successes are removed from its domain and given to another? And what becomes of the courageous soul that risked time and treasure, that painstakingly gathered evidence, that tracked down first hand accounts of sightings, that endured such ridicule and pity? That person is forced to drop the prefix from their title and join the mainstream scientific community. Whether or not this is a promotion or a demotion is a question I will leave up to the reader.

So please, my fellow cryptozoologists, heed the stories that follow. Remember them on those lonely nights in the field, during those times when you lose faith and begin to believe that maybe, just maybe, the skeptics are right.

CREATURES OLD...

I believe that many cryptids will be found to be not newly discovered creatures, but instead already known animals long thought to be extinct. Could the Loch Ness Monster turn out to be a surviving plesiosaur? Could the Thunderbird of North America really be a surviving pterosaur population? The possibility is not without precedent. The Arakan forest turtle of Myanmar was thought to be extinct since 1908, until it was rediscovered in 1994.[1] Now, although critically endangered, the animal can be seen in zoos throughout the world. The Javan elephant was believed to have gone extinct in the 1800s, until a population was discovered in Borneo in 2003.[2] While these animals went "extinct" relatively recently, there are also examples of the rediscovery of species that have been presumed to be extinct since prehistoric times.

The coelacanth is perhaps the most famous of these rediscoveries. An ancient fish known at first from only its fossil record, the coelacanth was thought to have gone extinct with the dinosaurs, at the end of the Cretaceous Period, roughly 65 million years ago. The zoological world was shocked when a living coelacanth turned up in a in a fisherman's net off the coast of South Africa in 1938.[3] Considering that people have been fishing off the coast of Africa for millennia, it is remarkable that the coelacanth remained hidden for so long. If the coelacanth could go undiscovered for thousands of years, what other "extinct" animals could still be lurking in the remote corners of Earth?

Perhaps the most intriguing animal that the mainstream scientific community believes to be extinct is Gigantopithecus. This genus was made up of three distinct species of giant ape living in Southeast Asia between 9 million to 100 thousand years ago. Standing 10 feet tall and weighing over 1,000 pounds, Gigantopithecus were the largest apes to have ever roamed our planet.[4] Interestingly, fossil evidence indicates these apes may have walked on two legs. It is possible that sightings of large, bipedal apes in the Himalayas and North America indicate surviving populations of Gigantopithecus. The Himalayas are a remote and rugged region. It is easy to see how a population of Gigantopithecus could survive there, rarely seen, and come to be known as the Yeti. It is also possible that a group of these apes crossed the Bering Land Bridge and became the Sasquatch of North America. When a Yeti or Sasquatch specimen is inevitably procured, one of the first analyses performed should be to compare the skeleton to fossils of Gigantopithecus to determine what their evolutionary relationship might be.

CREATURES NEW...

There are also those creatures that many consider too bizarre for belief: those creatures that sober, level-headed scientists cannot accept, no matter the number of firsthand accounts offered up by the uneducated masses. Animals like the platypus, the kangaroo, and the oarfish, all of which were at one point denied by the mainstream scientific community. Animals like the okapi.

The okapi is an animal native to Africa, specifically the Democratic Republic of the Congo. Standing about five feet tall and weighing over 500 pounds, this strange creature looks like a small giraffe with a shortened neck. It sports reddish brown fur on its body, but has black and white zebra-like stripes on all four of its legs. Although endangered, it is very much a real animal.

The okapi lives deep in the thick canopy forests of the Congo, and surely it has been long known to the inhabitants of the region. It was not described by European scientists, however, until 1901. And as we all know, if scientists have yet to describe something, it may as well not exist. The Africans who had been hunting these animals for centuries told European colonizers of their existence, but these firsthand accounts were written off as stories conflating multiple known animals into one mythical beast.

When Henry Morton Stanley, a Welsh colonialist, visited the Congo in 1887 on behalf of the Belgian government, he saw the okapi himself and sent his account of the animal back to Europe. This created a fair amount of excitement, as the account of a white colonialist was considered much more trustworthy than many accounts of African natives. But it was still not enough to convince skeptics of the existence of the okapi. Even fragments of hide sent to scientists by other European colonists were not enough to convince scientists that the okapi was real. It took a complete specimen and a description from an established zoologist to convince the world that the "Unicorn of the Congo" was real.[5]

Perhaps an even better example of the arrogance of Western Science is the Hoan Kiem turtle. The people of Vietnam have been telling tales of this animal for centuries. The legend states that Le Loi, the Vietnamese emperor who lead his people to independence from China in 1427, was boating on Hoan Kiem Lake when he encountered a diety in the form of a golden turtle. This turtle-god asked the emperor for the mystical sword that was given to him by the Dragon God King during the war with the Chinese. The supernatural turtle took the sword and disappeared into the water. In the centuries that followed, the Vietnamese continued to tell the story, and people occasionally reported sightings of the turtle. Western scientists dismissed the stories as legend and considered the Hoan Kiem turtle a mythical creature.

Then, in 1967, a fisherman caught a 200 pound, six foot long turtle with a gold colored abdomen. The specimen was preserved and displayed in a nearby temple. No further specimens were seen, and, despite the preserved and displayed body, scientists quickly returned the creature to the category of myth. I can only assume that the turtle from 1967 was considered a hoax, or that it was ignored in an act of cultural cognitive dissonance. Whatever the reason for the lack of belief in the Hoan Kiem turtle, irrefutable evidence surfaced in 1998, when a living specimen was captured on video and aired on Vietnamese television.[6] Sightings have occurred regularly since then and the Hoan Kiem turtle is now accepted by the scientific community.

It is worth noting that Hoan Kiem Lake is in the center of Hanoi, a city with a population of millions. Literally thousands of people walk along this lake, cross its bridges, and boat on its waters daily. Yet, even with all these watching eyes, the lake held its secret for five centuries. This should give pause to any skeptics who believe that there are just too many people on Earth for cryptids to live unnoticed.

The Burden of Proof

*Some people speak as if we were not justified in
rejecting a theological doctrine unless we can prove
it false. But the burden of proof does not lie upon
the rejecter....*

J.B. Bury

What, you may ask, is a quote expressing skepticism
concerning the existence of God doing in a field guide to
North America's cryptids? The quote is relevant not because of its theological skepticism, but because of the
reasoning behind its skepticism. This reasoning is not
limited to theology, nor is it limited to skeptics. The burden of proof is a nagging thought common to the minds
of the world's cryptozoologists. Cryptozoology draws

researchers into its fold for a variety of reasons. Some may have had an unexpected, life-changing encounter. Some may have an attraction to the mystery inherent in cryptid research. Some may want a deeper understanding of Earth's ecological systems, an understanding that takes into account all of its inhabitants, not simply the inhabitants recognized by mainstream science. Yet, despite their diverse backgrounds, most cryptozoologists share a common trait: the desire to find evidence that proves the existence of a particular cryptid and moves it out of the disreputable shadows and into the warm embrace of the mainstream biological sciences. If you are one such person, if your goal is not simply to see a cryptid, but to bring evidence of it to the general public, if you accept as yours the burden of proof, then you must be particularly observant and ever-ready to document your findings. The breakthroughs in cryptozoology will not arrive by chance, but through the meticulous efforts of prepared and hardworking individuals.

ANCILLARY EVIDENCE

Cryptids are physical, corporeal, substantive things, and, like all substantive things, they leave evidence of their existence for those who know how to find it. Cryptid sightings are, of course, incredibly rare. If sightings were commonplace, the creature would be acknowledged by mainstream science and it would not be classified as a cryptid.

A person who is able to recognize the ancillary signs of cryptid activity and focus their efforts on areas with a high likelihood of cryptid habitation will see their odds of an encounter increase dramatically. Recognizing, interpreting, and differentiating signs of megafauna is difficult and the subject warrants more space than it can be given here. Fortunately, hunters and wildlife biologists have written volumes on tracking game and serious students of cryptozoology would do well to study their work in addition to the information below.

Clues left by an animal for a tracker to find are known as "spoor." Spoor may include, but are not limited to: footprints, droppings, kills, drag marks, scratches, feathers, fur, dens, scents, sounds, trails, or even the behavior of other animals. The amount and quality of spoor available to a tracker is directly related to the observational skill and experience of said tracker. I recommend that novice cryptid researchers begin by learning to track a common animal similar to their cryptid of interest. For example, a cryptozoologist attempting to find Castoroides, the giant beaver, should be proficient in tracking *Castor canadensis,* the common beaver. This serves two purposes. First, the cryptid researcher learns to recognize spoor and begins to accumulate the experience necessary to be able to interpret it. Second, skeptics often write off cryptid sightings as cases of mistaken identity, and the cryptid researcher who is familiar with the spoor of the scientifically acknowledged animals of an area is in a better position to counter such claims.

It is important that the cryptid researcher carefully document any cryptid spoor that they encounter. Notes should be made, photographs should be taken, and, wherever possible, samples should be collected. Some of the strongest evidence supporting the famous Patterson-Gimlin Sasquatch film from 1967 are the casts of the footprints that were made after that incredible encounter. While not enough to convince a skeptic, the casts have proven invaluable to other Sasquatch researchers. The casts show a ridge in the arch of the foot, a trait that has been seen in casts of other Sasquatch footprints from various locations in North America.[7] Comparing these casts has allowed cryptozoologists to make predictions about the metatarsal anatomy of the Sasquatch that will be able to be tested when a specimen or skeleton is inevitably found.

PHOTOGRAPHIC EVIDENCE

The cryptozoologist attempting to document a cryptid encounter faces a great irony in that the photograph, the artifact that captures the encounter most accurately, is the artifact that will convince the fewest skeptics. While the adage says that seeing is believing, a long history of cryptozoological hoax photographs has dulled the public's appetite for belief. Furthermore, the contemporary ubiquity of photo-editing software has created a public that places little faith in the veracity of photographic images and is keenly skeptical of anyone that cannot offer more concrete evidence.

One of the earliest and most well known hoax photographs comes to us from the hills and dales of Yorkshire, in northern England. It was 1917, and 16-year-old Elsie Wright's family was hosting her nine-year-old cousin Frances Griffiths and her mother, Polly Wright, for the summer. The two girls spent many mornings playing near the small stream that ran behind the home in the small town of Cottingley, and they would often return to their parents with fanciful stories of the fairies that lived in the woods. On one such morning, Elsie borrowed her father's camera and took a photograph of her cousin sitting behind a rock while four fairies danced in front of her. The photograph, along with a second one showing Frances and a winged gnome, was developed by Elsie's father. Elsie was an artistic girl with experience working for a professional photographer, and her father believed, rightly, that the fairies were nothing more than cardboard cutouts.

Elsie's mother, on the other hand, evidently believed that the photographs were authentic evidence of the existence of fairies. Mrs. Wright had an interest in Theosophy, an esoteric religious philosophy that seeks knowledge of the divine through gnosis, the personal experience and understanding of supernatural truths. In 1919 she attended a meeting of the Bradford Theosophical Society and presented the photographs as evidence of the existence of fairies. Eventually the photographs made their way to Edward Gardner, who had them sent out to be examined by various authorities, including experts from the Kodak corporation.

The results were mixed, with some analysts believing the photographs to be authentic and others remaining unconvinced. Many members of the public, however, wholeheartedly believed in the veracity of the photographs. Among those who counted themselves as believers was the author Sir Arthur Conan Doyle. Doyle, famous for creating the intrepid Sherlock Holmes, was an adamant spiritualist with an interest in all things metaphysical.

Doyle and Gardner wanted very much to prove to the world that these Cottingley Fairies were real, so much so that they stopped thinking critically and allowed themselves to be further taken in by the two girls. Armed with cameras for the girls, Gardner visited Frances and Elsie in July of 1920. The girls convinced Gardner that the fairies would not appear in front of a presumably untrustworthy stranger, and Gardner stayed back with the Wrights while the girls went down to the stream to take more photographs. The girls, of course, were successful in attracting the fairies, giving Gardner and Doyle the new evidence that they so desperately wanted.

Doyle published the photographs in *The Strand*, a monthly general interest magazine. The public's reaction was again split. The skeptics were many and vocal, but believers, perhaps still naive regarding the young girls' ability or desire to fake a photograph, were convinced. It wasn't until 1983, long after Sir Arthur Conan Doyle's death in 1930, that the girls admitted the fairies were indeed nothing more than cardboard cutouts.[8] How many skeptics the girls created out of people who would otherwise be cryptozoological believers is unknown.

Another famous hoax photograph, the 1934 "Surgeon's Photograph" of the Loch Ness Monster, is perhaps far more damaging to the reputations of the world's cryptozoologists. Robert Kenneth Wilson, a London doctor, was credited with having taken the now famous photograph showing the dark silhouette of Nessie's neck arching out of the waters of the Loch. Published in the *Daily Mail* on April 21st, 1934, it was long held up as the finest evidence of the existence of the Loch Ness Monster.[9]

We now know that the photograph was the work of one Marmaduke Wetherell, an employee of the *Daily Mail.* Wetherell held a grudge against his employers due to the ridicule he suffered concerning his outspoken belief in the Loch Ness Monster. Assisted by three others, he built a small model of the monster on top of a toy submarine and photographed it close up, so as to crop out the shore line and obscure any attempt to discern the scale of the creature. He then gave the photographic plates to Robert Kenneth Wilson, presumably to hide the photograph's provenance from his employers and to take advantage of the credibility afforded to members of the mainstream medical community.

It is no wonder that, after having been exposed to countless hoaxes such as these, most members of the public are unwilling to accept photographs as authentic evidence of cryptids. What then, is the honest cryptozoologist to do? I believe that it is still very important for cryptozoologists to take as many photographs, or, even better, videos, as they are able. While these images will almost certainly be explained away by skeptics, they can offer important clues to other cryptozoological researchers. They may capture how the creature moves, how it attempts to camouflage itself to avoid detection, or how it responds to encounters with humans. Whenever possible, frame your photo so that the scale of the creature can be determined by comparing it to some other object of known or measurable size. Photos and videos are invaluable resources. Any one photo may provide the piece of evidence that leads a researcher to the Holy Grail of cryptozoology, the one thing that even the most stringent skeptic would be forced to accept: cryptid DNA.

GENETIC EVIDENCE

First hand accounts, footprint castings, and photographs are all exciting evidence and can do much to advance the conversation among cryptozoologists, but they alone are not enough to change any minds in the mainstream scientific community. For these hardened skeptics, the only evidence that matters is genetic evidence. Anything short of a body or tissue sample is sure to be written off as either the work of a dishonest huckster or the wishful thinking of a foolish believer.

If the cryptozoologist is lucky enough to come across an already deceased cryptid body, the body should be collected and preserved through refrigeration. It is irresponsible, however, for anyone to kill a cryptid for the purpose of obtaining a specimen. Though reliable estimates of cryptid populations are nearly impossible to arrive at, we can all agree that they are extremely rare and any human behaviors that further lower the population should be avoided.

This leaves the responsible cryptozoologist with the task of collecting a tissue sample from a living cryptid for DNA analysis. Collecting DNA from a living, and likely unwilling, creature is no small feat. The sample obtained must be collected in a way that minimizes the probability of contamination, both from other animals and from the researcher. The most reliable way to do this by collecting cells from inside the cryptid's cheek with a sterile buccal swab kit.[10] A buccal swab kit should contain sterile gloves, a sterile cotton swab, and a sterile collection bag. The researcher should swab the inside of the creature's mouth for approximately eight seconds, then immediately transfer the swab to the sterile collection bag, taking care not to touch the swab to anything else or to contaminate the swab by coughing or sneezing on it. The downside of this method is that it requires the researcher to capture and subdue the cryptid, which may be prohibitively dangerous.

A second method of collecting DNA is by gathering hair or fur samples. If a cryptid is captured for buccal swabbing, a hair sample should be taken as well. Otherwise, hair may be gathered from wherever it is found. Note that the DNA for analysis is not found in the hair itself, but in the tissue surrounding the base of the hair. If possible, multiple hairs with tissue intact should be collected. Remember to use sterile technique and avoid contaminating the sample. If neither of these two options is available, the researcher can use any available sample to attempt DNA analysis. This could be found blood, spit, phlegm, skin, or semen. While these samples are better than nothing, the chances of them being contaminated are greater than the chances of a sample taken directly from a subject using sterile technique. As a last resort, urine and feces should be collected if they are found, but contamination is almost assured as urine soaks into wherever it lands and feces is high in bacteria.

Once a sample of cryptid DNA is collected, it needs to be sequenced. While the cost of gene sequencing has come down dramatically in recent years, the process requires specialized knowledge and equipment, and is therefore not within the domain of the home researcher. The best way to have DNA sequenced is to contact the biology department at a local college or university and find someone willing to help navigate the process. Partnering with an experienced biologist will also be beneficial when it comes to presenting findings to the public. Not only are members of the public more likely to take seriously a team with connections to a reputable institution, but an experienced biologist will be an incredible asset when it comes to analyzing the DNA sequence and getting the research published and peer reviewed.

At this point I would like to make clear my relationship with the mainstream scientific community. I fear the reader may get the impression that I believe science has nothing to offer the cryptozoologist, when in fact, nothing could be further from the truth. Contemporary biology is a fascinating field, one in which exciting new discoveries are being made nearly everyday. Cryptozoologists have much to learn from studying the work of biologists, ecologists, and other scientists. Furthermore, as definitive evidence of the existence of cryptids is discovered, we will be able to probe every facet of the lives of these intriguing creatures using techniques developed and tested over centuries by a multitude of gifted and dedicated scientists.

I do take issue, however, with the scientific community's unwillingness to take the field of cryptozoology seriously. No matter how convincing a cryptozoologist's evidence, it is very difficult to convince a biologist to partner on cryptid research. And without partnering with someone associated with a reputable institution, it is very difficult to get research published in a reputable journal. DNA sequencing is available commercially, and cryptid researchers may be forced to take this route. I strongly suggest that once a cryptid sample is sequenced the information be made public by whatever means possible. Analyzing a DNA sequence will require the help of many people, and if the evidence is ever to be accepted it must be available for all to review.

Cryptid Safety

Rare is the person who, after reading about some first hand cryptid encounter, is content to remain within the confines of their home, studying the world's cryptids from the safety of their couch. Yes, once bitten by the cryptid bug, most people are eager to get out into the field and attempt to make thrilling discoveries of their own. Some are a little too eager. Over just the past decade, nearly two dozen cryptid researchers have been killed while performing field research across the globe.[11] Sadly, nearly all of these deaths could have been avoided. Cryptozoological field research often involves working with unpredictable large animals in remote locations. Due to the danger inherent to the field, it would be irresponsible to not say a few things here about both cryptid and backcountry safety.

BACKCOUNTRY SAFETY

Serious attempts to view a live cryptid will often require extended travel in remote, sometimes even wilderness, locations. It is easy for the cryptozoologist, eager to learn as much as possible about their quarry, to overlook learing how to stay safe in the wild. There are many dangers confronting anyone who ventures into the backcountry. The good news is that most of these dangers can be very effectively minimized with a little planning.

Every expedition into the backcountry requires its own set of equipment and skills. A cryptozoologist searching for a Chupacabra in the Arizona desert, for example, will need to prepare differently than a cryptozoologist looking for a Sasquatch in the forests of British Columbia.

There is, however, a list of ten items that those experienced in traveling through the backcountry agree are of particular importance. No researcher undertaking a journey into a wilderness area for any period of time should be without them. The items on this list are essential, but not sufficient. There are other items that will be necessary depending on your particular needs

The Ten Essentials

1. A magnetic compass and topographic map
2. A flashlight
3. Extra clothing
4. A pocket knife
5. A spaceblanket
6. Extra food and water
7. Matches in a waterproof container
8. A firestarter
9. A first aid kit
10. Sun protection

and the conditions of the area you will be exploring. It is better to carry more than you need than to be in want while far from civilization.

Merely possessing these tools is not enough to ensure safety in the backcountry. It is vitally important that anyone venturing into the wilderness knows how to use all of their potentially lifesaving equipment well before an emergency arises. Practice making fires at home rather than trying to figure it out under cold, wet, and stressful conditions. Bring extra flashlight batteries and know how to install them. Learn how to use a topographic map and compass. Consider studying the terrain and landmarks of the area before a journey begins and reference your map to see how they are represented. I am always surprised at the number of hikers I come across who have wisely packed a compass and map but haven't the faintest clue as to how to use them.

It is also essential that everyone venturing into the backcountry leaves a detailed and dated itinerary with a friend or family member. If you fail to return by the noted date, search and rescue crews will know the general area to search. If you do not leave information about where you will be traveling, you WILL NOT be found and will need to rely solely on your own skills to return you to safety.

Hypothermia is one of the biggest dangers lurking in the wilderness, killing almost 1,500 Americans annually. It is essential that the clothing worn into the wilderness keeps the wearer both warm and dry. This is best accomplished by dressing in layers. The layers closest to the skin should be thin and breathable to avoid becoming soaked in perspiration. Cotton should be avoided because it does not hold heat when wet. High quality, soft wool is the best choice. Middle layers should be heavier to provide warmth, but still able to wick moisture away from the skin. Again, cotton is to be avoided. The outermost layer should provide warmth and be completely waterproof. Modern fabrics able to repel water while letting vapor from the inside work its way out are worth seeking for outer layers. To stay dry, simply remove a layer before becoming soaked with sweat. To stay warm, simply add another layer when necessary.

When in the backcountry, your supply of fresh drinking water should always be in the back of your mind. Even when not taxing their bodies, humans need eight cups of water daily. Hiking through the wilderness is sure to increase that requirement. Water is heavy and even the strongest hiker is unlikely to be able to carry all of the water they will need. There are a few ways to purify water for drinking. Sterilization tablets are cheap, lightweight, and easy to use. The downside is that they can leave an unpleasant taste in the water. Hand activated pumps that filter water leave water tasting clean and fresh, but they are more expensive, heavier, and require more effort. Purifiers that use UV light as a sterilizing agent are light and easy to use, but require batteries to operate. The method chosen is not as important as ensuring that a purification method is available. With a little planning, any cryptozoologist should be able to avoid the risk of unpurified water. While diarrhea at home is unpleasant, diarrhea in the backcountry can quickly cause dehydration and lead to death.

Backcountry safety is something to take seriously, and no person should travel alone in the wilderness without extensive experience. To build experience, start with short day hikes in areas frequented by other people. These short trips are also excellent opportunities to hone animal tracking skills. Learning from others is often the quickest way to gain knowledge, so consider joining a camping or hiking group. Many outfitters offer courses for beginning backpackers, and there is plenty of good information available online or at a public library. Do not overestimate your own skills and do not get yourself into situations that you cannot get out of.

CRYPTID SAFETY

An encounter with a cryptid can be a worrisome experience. Cryptids are often larger and stronger than the people who encounter them, and because sightings are rare, little is known about their behavior. Furthermore, cryptozoologists often attempt to pursue and observe their quarry while remaining unknown to the animal. This can lead to sudden, unexpected encounters with sometimes disastrous results. As a general rule, a scared animal is a dangerous animal, and care should be taken to avoid surprising a cryptid.

Fortunately, cryptids are reclusive by their very nature. The scarcity of prolonged sightings is evidence that these animals would much rather run and hide than confront a human being. Nearly all of the documented cryptid sightings are short affairs, with the cryptid quickly slinking off to cover shortly after being sighted. Your greatest concern will likely not be keeping the cryptid from becoming aggressive, but keeping the cryptid around long enough for you to document the encounter.

Still, you may find yourself in close proximity to a creature that is unhappy to have been found, and in such situations you will need to have a ready strategy for de-escalation. Throughout my many years of cryptid research I have had numerous personal encounters with cryptids. These encounters have led me to a general principle that guides my behavior in situations where a cryptid is agitated and possibly dangerous. Please note that this is a guideline developed through my own anecdotal experience for my own personal use, and I cannot guarantee the behavior of any cryptid. These are unpredictable creatures and anyone in their presence should exercise utmost caution.

All cryptid species exist somewhere along a fairly broad continuum of intellectual ability. Near the bottom of this continuum are those creatures like the Chupacabra, animals with simple, primitive, reptilian brains. With these creatures, the best strategy is to make yourself appear larger and more intimidating. Stand up straight, extend your arms, and open your jacket if you are wearing one. You may wave your arms and make loud noises, but do not make any movements that could be interpreted as an attack. Your goal should be to appear intimidating to the animal, but not to be an immediate threat. It is also advisable to face the creature and to maintain eye contact.

The strategy for dealing with creatures on the other end of the intelligence continuum is different. Perhaps you come across an animal with a highly developed, human-like brain, such as a Sasquatch. Your goal should not be to appear intimidating. Creatures of greater intelligence are more likely to correctly assess the situation and will not be fooled by your false show of strength. If you meet such a creature, do not make any sudden movements. Maintain a non-threatening body posture by angling your body slightly away from the animal and avoiding direct eye contact. If you need to put more distance between the animal and yourself, back away slowly. These creatures offer your best chance for an extended cryptid encounter, provided you can prove that you are not a threat.

Notes on Nomenclature

Due to the unwillingness of the mainstream scientific community to acknowledge and study cryptids, most of these animals have not been given proper scientific names. This has caused much confusion as cryptozoologists have been left to determine their own conventions with regard to cryptid nomenclature. This guide attempts to follow the conventions developed by serious cryptid researchers, some of which differ from standard scientific usage. In order to avoid confusion, these conventions are outlined below.

The first unusual cryptid convention is the tendency for both cryptozoologists and the general public to refer to an entire cryptid species as a singular individual. It is common, for example, to hear that the Chupacabra is responsible for livestock deaths across southern North America. This does not mean that there is a single, individual goat-sucker roaming the countryside. Rather, the singular title "Chupacabra" stands in euphemistically for the entire population of Chupacabras. It is important for the reader to remember that all of the cryptids represented in this book are members of breeding populations and are not lone individuals. They are not monsters. They are subject to the same biological, ecological, and genetic laws that apply to all living things.

The second convention worth noting is that cryptid names are capitalized while the common names of more widely accepted animals are not. This, unfortunately, likely contributes to the misconception that cryptids are individual monsters and not members of large breeding populations. I do not doubt that some cryptozoologists will take issue with my decision to not insist that cryptid names follow standard scientific protocol. Many people believe that to do otherwise delegitimizes the entire field of cryptozoology. I believe that the best way for cryptozoologists to deal with this is not to engage in the sisyphean task of insisting that cryptids be treated just like all other animals when it comes to naming, but instead to redouble our efforts to provide the world with irrefutable evidence of their existence so that these magnificent creatures can be seen as legitimate in all aspects of their lives.

I also do not doubt that some will take issue with the cryptids included, or, more likely, not included, in this guide. I have attempted to include all of the legitimate cryptids of North America, but not those creatures that are supernatural or paranormal in origin. It is not always an easy task to determine whether a specific report concerns a genuine encounter with a population of undiscovered but truly corporeal animals or is simply a hackneyed retelling of supernatural lore. The task is further complicated by fact that encounters with rare animals are often unexpected, brief, and startling for the people involved. Paranormal traits can be attributed to even widely-accepted animals under such circumstances. In those situations where the cryptozoological jury is out with regards to the legitimacy of an animal, I have included the species, thinking it better to err on the side of providing more information to the reader than less.

Aquatic Cryptids

ALABAMA CREEPER

The Alabama Creeper is a creature misnamed, as it has been found exclusively in the sinkholes, disappearing streams, and underwater caves of southern Florida. The limestone that makes up the bedrock in most of Florida is porous and extremely susceptible to erosion by rainwater. This erosion has created what is known as Karst Topography, an incredible underwater drainage system that is home to the Alabama Creeper.[12] It is not known why a creature found in Florida is named for a neighboring state.

No person is known to have seen an Alabama Creeper in its entirety. The creature keeps the bulk of its body underground in its limestone home, sending just a tentacle or two out onto dry land to capture prey. The tentacles of the Alabama Creeper are narrow, often being described as the thickness of a roll of quarters. The skin is a mottled brown and the bottom of the tentacle is lined with suckers. When disturbed, the Alabama Creeper quickly retreats to its underground sanctuary.

Every documented sighting of the Alabama Creeper has occurred in the hour immediately before or immediately after sunrise. The high level of prey activity in conjunction with the low intensity of the tentacle-dehydrating sun make this the prime time of day for the Creeper to hunt. Alabama Creeper tentacles are often seen repeatedly in the same location, leading to speculation that once the creature finds a niche to inhabit it remains largely immobile, save for the creeping tentacles it sends onto dry land. The best strategy for finding a complete Creeper would be to carefully follow the tentacle back to where it emerges from its watery, subterranean home and carefully excavate the area. Tread carefully and note that the tentacles are highly sensitive. It is believed that the Alabama Creeper is extremely sensitive to vibrations in the ground and will quickly retreat if the cryptozoologist does not walk with the most delicate of steps.

An excellent place to search for leads would be any South Florida baitshop. Many sightings come to us from fishermen whose prefered style of fishing is to cast live bait into inland waters and wait paitently for a fish to bite.

ALTAMAHA-HA

The Altamaha-ha is a large aquatic cryptid that inhabits the tangled maze of streams and channels at the mouth of the Altamaha River on the Atlantic coast of

Altamaha-ha

southeastern Georgia. Eyewitnesses describe the creature as up to 30 feet in length with a dark, tread-like pattern on its greenish skin that blends well with the brackish waters of its estuary home. The animal's head is shaped roughly like that of an alligator, but the snout is shorter and the nostrils are described as "human," or "ape-like." The Altamaha-ha propels itself through the water by moving its flat tail in an up and down motion, similar to a seal or a whale, but unlike a fish or a shark.

Cryptozoologists searching for the Altamaha-ha would do well to begin their search in the town of Darien, Georgia. Located about 60 miles down the coast from Savannah and at the mouth of the Altamaha River, it is an easy place to rent a boat. The mouth of the Altamaha is a marsh crisscrossed by river channels and old rice canals, and people unfamiliar with the area should bring a good map, or better yet, hire a guide. Do not confuse sightings of alligators, manatees, stumps, or whales with true sightings of the Altamaha-ha.

ANGEOA

The Angeoa is a mysterious aquatic creature inhabiting Dubawnt Lake in Nunavut, Canada. It is thought to be an extremely large black whale or fish with a massive dorsal fin. The beast is rarely seen, since Dubawnt Lake is large, its shores are uninhabited, and it is covered with ice for 10 months of the year. Most sightings are from Inuit fishermen who describe it as being from 40 to 60 feet long. If the Angeoa is a whale, it would be the first known freshwater whale. Cryptozoologists hunting the Angeoa will want to focus their efforts on places where the creature would be able to come through the ice to breathe. The Angeoa is considered aggressive and has been known to sink kayaks and canoes. Exercise extreme caution. The icy waters of Dubawnt Lake can quickly cause hypothermia, turning a usually benign canoe capsizing into a potentially fatal experience.

BLOOP

The Bloop is the name given to a mysterious audio recording from the Pacific Ocean that may indicate the presence of a large, unknown sea creature. In 1997, two listening stations in the Pacific Ocean operated by the National Oceanic and Atmospheric Administration picked up a very loud, ultra-low frequency sound.[13] Analysis of the sound indicated that it was not man-made, nor was it similar to common geological events. The sound is often described as "organic."

The blue whale is the largest and loudest scientifically accepted animal. The Bloop recording is several times louder than the blue whale. This indicates that the Bloop was made by an animal that is, at the very least, louder than the blue whale, and quite possibly larger. The Bloop is not the only unidentified recording made public by NOAA. Other equally mysterious recordings have been named Julia, Upsweep, Whistle, Slowdown, and Train.

The estimate for the origin of The Bloop is alarmingly close to the coordinates given by H.P. Lovecraft as the location of the sunken city of R'lyeh, home to the sea monster Cthulhu.

CASTOROIDES

The Pleistocene Epoch, from roughly 2.5 million years ago to ten thousand years ago, was a golden time for North American mammals. Native horses and camels, now extinct, roamed the Great Plains in huge herds. Saber-toothed cats fed on the abundant supply of mammoths and mastodons. There were armadillos the size of cars and sloths the size of elephants. The end of

Castoroides sp.

the Pleistocene brought about a massive extinction. Entire branches of the mammalian tree were lost. Castoroides is a Pleistocene genus of beaver that the mainstream scientific community believes went extinct in that late Pleistocene extinction event.[14] These beavers were much larger than modern beavers, reaching six feet in length. They were otherwise similar in appearance to modern beavers, though the hind feet were proportionally smaller and the tail was proportionally longer. The teeth of Castoroides also differ from the teeth of modern beavers, leading some scientists to speculate that the ancient beaver did not fell trees and create dams the way that contemporary beavers do. Though officially extinct, reports of Castoroides still emerge from northern Minnesota and southern Ontario.

The Boundary Waters Wilderness Canoe Area in Minnesota along with Quetico Provincial Park in Ontario provide over 2 million acres of unspoiled wilderness. Carved and gouged by glaciers, this wilderness is covered by a network of lakes, streams and bogs. It is the perfect habitat for Castoroides. The first reports of giant beavers date to the 1920s and coincide with increased human presence in the Boundary Waters region. As recreational use of the area increased, so did sightings of Castoroides, reaching a peak of nearly a dozen sightings a year in the 1970s. Encounters with Castoroides are now rare in the southern portions of the Boundary Waters region, with most reports coming from the northern reaches of Quetico Provincial Park. It is speculated that climate change has shifted the range of Castoroides northward.

FRESHWATER SHARK

Unlike most of the other creatures on this list, the Freshwater Shark is well-known and accepted in the scientific community. However, individual reports of encounters are nearly always met with skepticism and disbelief, earning the animal the title of cryptid.

The only North American shark able to tolerate freshwater is the bull shark.[15] This shark has the ability to osmoregulate, that is, it has to ability to maintain a stable concentration of electrolytes and water within its cells, regardless of the salinity of the water in which it is swimming. Most other sharks do not have this ability. In a freshwater environment water will flow into the shark's cells, causing the cells to burst and kill the shark.

Bull sharks are large, apex predators. The females are slightly larger than the males and can reach 11 feet in length and over 500 pounds in weight. The sharks have stocky, gray bodies with white underbellies. The bull shark's preference for warm, shallow waters and its unusually high testosterone levels have led to a relatively high number of human fatalities. The bull shark is the third most common species of shark responsible for attacks on humans, behind the great white and the tiger shark.

As large carnivores, bull sharks require a fairly large body of water to provide them with enough food. This prevents them from surviving in many of the smaller

lakes they may be introduced to after coastal flooding.
Freshwater bull shark habitat is further limited by the
animal's requirement for warm water. This is the reason
that the Great Lakes and the St. Lawrence Seaway, which
would otherwise be prime places to look for for

Freshwater Shark

Freshwater Sharks, are uninhabited by bull sharks. The majority of freshwater bull shark sightings occur in the brackish estuaries and river deltas of the southeastern United States. The fish may travel deep inland provided that the river is large enough. Bull sharks have been caught as far north as Illinois on the Mississippi River.

FUR-BEARING TROUT

Stories of furry fish date back to the 1600s, when European explorers returned with marvelous tales of the New World and the animals found there, but there have been no credible specimens discovered to date. The Fur-Bearing Trout lives on, however, with taxidermied chimeras being found in gift shops and gag shops worldwide. The stories may have gotten their start from a species of cotton mold that can infect living fish, covering them in a layer of white, hair-like fibers.[16]

GIANT ANACONDA

The green anaconda is the world's heaviest snake, and may be the world's longest. The longest scientifically accepted Anaconda measured 17 feet, but it is likely that much larger specimens exist. Length measurements in excess of 20 feet are common in historical reports, and the anaconda's remote habitat of swamps and streams deep in the Amazon rainforest make obtaining accurate measurements difficult.

Green anacondas entered the United States as pets. As their owners tired of their snakes, or the snakes became too large for comfort, many were released into the wild. Some of these snakes were lucky enough to slither into the perfect habitat, the Everglades of southern Florida, and there are now breeding populations of the snakes living in that vast swamp.[17] Anacondas in the everglades have been reported at over 30 feet in length and two feet in diameter.

Giant Anaconda

GIANT CATFISH

It is not uncommon for a local fishing hole to breed tales of monstrously large fish, but there is strong evidence that for a stretch of the Mississippi River near the Louisiana-Arkansas border, the stories are true.

Catfish can grow to gargantuan proportions. The Mekong giant catfish of Southeast Asia can grow in excess of 600 pounds. Some species in South America are not far behind. There are even species of catfish, the goonch catfish of south Asia and the wels of Europe, that are known to eat small children. The largest recognized catfish in North America, the blue catfish and the flathead catfish, are much smaller, rarely topping 100 pounds. There are, however, unconfirmed reports of catfish growing to a significantly larger size.

The most credible report of a monstrous catfish comes from divers working on the construction of the Benjamin G. Humphreys bridge. Built in 1940, this bridge crosses the Mississippi River and connects the towns of Lake Village, Arkansas and Greenville, Mississippi. In October of 1939, a team of divers plunged into the murky waters of the river to inspect the pilings supporting the still under construction bridge. They surfaced sooner than expected and refused to go back down, citing an enormous catfish the size of a city bus. All three of the divers walked away from the project, preferring the loss of their jobs to another encounter with the terrifying fish. Just a few years later, in 1947, a tugboat captain pushing a barge upriver reported seeing "a large, dark shape just below the surface of the water. It must have been the size of a whale." No more sightings of the fish were made until the early 1960s, when three separate fishing boats were overturned and their occupants nearly drowned. One victim reported that the creature that tipped his boat was "larger than I thought could live in that river."

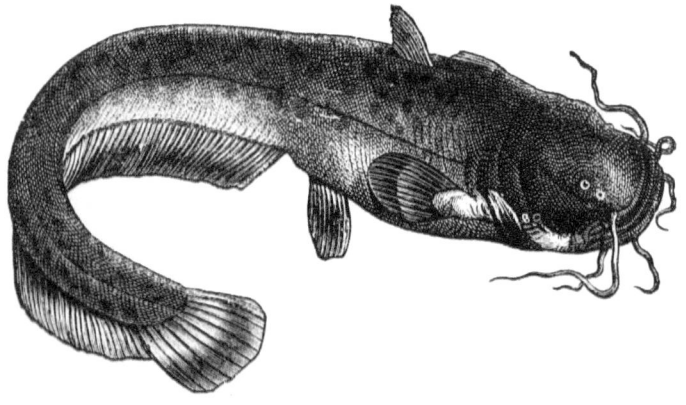

Giant Catfish

Catfish lifespans are measured in decades, and it is likely that this particular fish is no longer alive. But if the lower Mississippi River was able to produce one extremely large fish, it is probable that there are others lurking in the deep, dark holes of this massive river. Once again, the best place to begin your search is local baitshops. Be advised, the best fishing holes are closely guarded secrets, and catfishermen will likely be reticent to share information with outsiders.

GIANT DRAGONFISH

There is still much we don't know about what lives in the ocean, but it is easy to forget that a mere 100 years ago, we knew almost nothing. That began to change when William Beebe and Otis Barton took to the depths in their audacious bathysphere, a claustrophobic steel sphere lowered into the ocean on a cable. Prior to Beebee and Barton's bathysphere, ocean explorers used open-bottomed diving bells and diving helmets to explore the ocean but were limited to depths under 100 feet. Using their new invention, Beebe and Barton were able to descend over 3,000 feet. The pair made a series of dives

Beebe and Barton with their Bathysphere

in Bermuda from 1930 to 1934. They were able to observe and describe many creatures never before seen, but the most intriguing was the Giant Dragonfish.

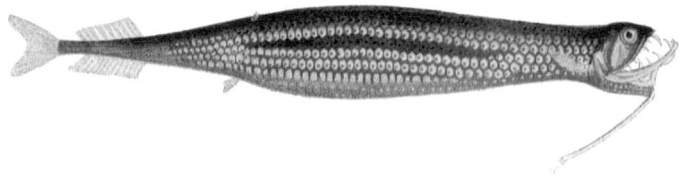

Giant Dragonfish

Dragonfish are typically small, deep-sea fish, rarely reaching 10 inches in length. They have large jaws with disproportionately large teeth. Trailing below a dragonfish is a long barbel with a bioluminescent tip. The fish uses this glowing blue appendage to lure even smaller fish into its waiting jaws. While nearly 3000 feet beneath the surface of the ocean, off the coast of Nonsuch Island in Bermuda, Beebe and Barton encountered a creature identical to the common dragonfish in every way but its size. This terrifying creature was estimated to be six feet long. Beebe named the animal *Bathysphere intacta*. It has not been seen since, and remains unrecognized by science.

GIGLIOLI'S WHALE

While sailing off of the coast of Chile in 1867, Italian zoologist Enrico Hillyer Giglioli encountered a whale that he was not familiar with. He described the animal as a large baleen whale but without the usual throat pleats, having unusual sickle shaped flippers, and, most notably, having two dorsal fins located about six feet apart.[18] Similar whales have since been sighted near France and Scotland, indicating a global distribution.

Giglioli's Whale

LAKE MONSTER

Lake monsters are the most commonly sighted cryptids, not just in North America, but worldwide. The most recognizable feature of a lake monster is its long neck ending in a small, hydrodynamic head. The body is wide, flat, and is adorned with posterior and anterior flippers and a long tail. The skin of a lake monster is smooth and muted in color. Length estimates vary considerably, with reports ranging from 30 to 90 feet. These length discrepancies are probably due to rarity of complete lake monster sightings. Often only the head or the back of the creature is visible.

The similarity of lake monsters to Plesiosaurs has led some to believe that the ancient marine reptiles are not extinct, but merely low in population and reduced in range to deep, cold, fresh-water lakes. Skeptics attribute lake monster sightings to a variety of commonplace phenomena, from boat wakes crossing and forming unusual patterns to groups of otters swimming in formation. Some people speculate that lake monster sightings are in fact sightings of a large, unidentified fresh-water eel.

Lake Monster

The most famous lake monster is the Loch Ness Monster, in northern Scotland, but cryptozoologists do not have to leave North America to search for one. Lake Champlain in the Northeastern United States is famous for housing Champ, and Lake Simcoe in Ontario is home to the often sighted Igopogo. Other, less-famous lake monsters live in Bear Lake, Iliamna Lake, Lake Manitoba, Lake Memphremagog, Lake Minnetonka, Muskrat Lake,

Okanagan Lake, Payette Lake, Lake Winnibigoshish, Lake Tahoe, Turtle Lake, all five Great Lakes, and the St. Lawrence Seaway.

LUSCA

The Lusca is a cryptid native to the Caribbean Sea. It is thought to be an octopus of colossal proportions. The largest octopus recognized by mainstream science had a length of 11 feet, the Lusca is estimated to be anywhere between 30 and 100 feet in length. The Lusca is morphologically similar to other octopuses, and it has exhibited the ability to change color to blend in with its surroundings.

The Lusca lives at the edge of the continental shelf and in the deep sinkholes that dot the Caribbean Sea's limestone floor. Partially decomposed carcasses of dead Lusca have washed ashore in Florida and the Bahamas, with one particular specimen even containing a gigantic beak. Sightings have been reported throughout the Caribbean, with the highest concentration centered on Andros, an island in the Bahamas.

Skeptics claim that the Lusca is simply a misidentified giant squid. The giant squid is a very real animal, but only rarely seen, and it was only photographed in the wild in 2004. While it is indeed likely that some Lusca sightings can be attributed to misidentified giant squid, there are a handful of reports that contain details indicating otherwise. Most notable among these is a 1671 report from British explorer William Dampier, who claimed to have seen a giganitc octopus crawl up the side of his ship while it was moored off of the coast of Jamaica. The creature then grabbed two crew members with its tentacles and devoured them after returning to the sea.

Lusca

MEGALODON

The Megalodon is a species of shark very similar to the great white shark in general appearance, but much larger in size. While the great white shark is a fearsome predator at 20 feet in length, the Megalodon can grow to a truly terrifying 60 feet long. The Megalodon came onto the scene roughly 16 million years ago, just before the appearance of the first hominids. The mainstream scientific community believes that the Megalodon went extinct about 1.5 million years ago, but there is evidence to suggest otherwise.

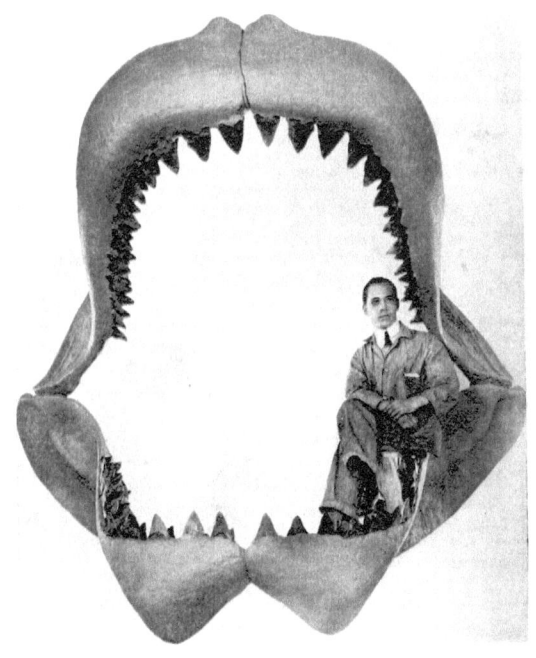

Fossil Jaws from Megalodon

The Megalodon, like all sharks, has a skeleton composed primarily of cartilage, which is poorly preserved in the fossil record. This means that the majority of the evidence of the existence of Megalodon comes from teeth, jaw bones, and central vertebra. Fossils of these bones have been found all over the world, and are usually dated to over 1.5 million years ago. Usually, but not always.

In 1872 the British Royal Navy sent the HMS Challenger on a voyage to study the ocean. The ship was set up with an array of scientific equipment, including netting to dredge the deepest parts of the sea floor and document the findings. It was on this voyage that the crew succeeded in measuring the deepest point in the world's oceans, a location named The Challenger Deep, near Guam in the Pacific Ocean. Not far from here the crew also recovered a Megalodon tooth from the sea floor. In 1959 this tooth was analyzed by Dr. W. Tschernezky at Queen Mary College in London and found to be only 10,000 years old. Other teeth have been found by Chinese commercial dredging companies that have been estimated to be about 40,000 years old. These dates indicate that Megalodon was still hunting the oceans when modern humans were discovering agriculture.

Sharks are ancient creatures, and are exceptionally resistant to change. It is very possible that a population of Megalodons has survived, living at the fringes of human exploration, feasting on sperm whales and giant squid in the blackness of the deep.

MERPEOPLE

Mermaids and Mermen are among the most ancient and universal of all cryptids. For as long as there have been sailors, there have been sightings of these half-fish, half-human creatures. Homer likely based his Sirens on stories of Merpeople, and they appear in the ancient Arabic tale of Scheherazade. They were portents of ill-fortune in medieval Britain, and Hans Christian Andersen wrote a story about a diminutive Mermaid that remains popular with children today. Traditional Chinese stories tell of a Mermaid whose tears become pearls, and the Mermaid Suvannamaccha is a popular character in Cambodian and Thai stories.

Mermaid and Merman

In North America, the most famous Merpeople are the ones described by Christopher Columbus in 1493. Just before Columbus left the New World to return to

Europe his personal journal recounts a rather strange event. He writes about "three female forms" rising out of the water to observe his boats. As an experienced sailor, Columbus would have been at the very least familiar with stories of Mermaids, and had possibly seen other Mermaids himself off the coast of Africa. In any event, he seems to take the sighting in stride, and the episode merits only a brief entry in his journal. Columbus was not the only well-known historical figure to see Merpeople in the Caribbean. Many pirate crews reported seeing Mermaids. Even the fearless Blackbeard seemed uncomfortable with their presence, and he made a point of avoiding waters known to be inhabited by Merpeople.

The long history of Merpeople sightings has provided fertile ground for hoaxers. The astute cryptozoologist will be wary of preserved specimens and so-called "Fijian Mermaids." These are simply taxidermic chimeras made from the head and torso of a monkey and the tail of a fish. P.T. Barnum was known to possess one and there is a famous example on display at a general store in Calgary, Alberta.

Fijian Mermaid

RHINOCEROS DOLPHIN

The Rhinoceros Dolphin is a species of dolphin with two dorsal fins, similar to Giglioli's Whale. Unlike Giglioli's whale, the Rhinoceros Dolphin has not been described as differing from the common dolphin in any way other than its extra fin. It is likely that reports of the Rhinoceros Dolphin are due to a trick of the eye, with two dolphins, one in front of the other, appearing as one. It is also possible that some sightings are due to genetically mutated individuals, and not to a truly separate species of dolphin.

SEA SERPENT

If you dig deep enough in any coastal town, you will unearth at least one story of a sea serpent. If you can't find an old sailor who has seen one first-hand, you will at least be able to find one who knows someone who saw one, once, when they were young. These monsters come in all shapes and sizes. Some are described as looking like long-necked plesiosaurs, others as giant sea lions. Reports have been made of gargantuan ocean-dwelling centipedes, or larger than life turtles, or eels. Most of these sightings can be attributed to misidentification of rare, but well documented animals. A frilled shark would look bizarre to someone who has never seen such a creature, as would an oarfish. And it would be easy to exaggerate the size of an elephant seal after seeing the 16 foot beast for the first time. There are, however, two famous sea serpents that are worth noting. One is from the Atlantic, and one is from the Pacific. Both remain unexplained.

The Maliseet and the Passamaquoddy tribes were the first people to record encountering a sea serpent off the rocky coast of New England. The monster, which they named Apotamkin, lived in Passamaquoddy Bay and was reported to devour anyone unlucky enough to cross paths with it. When Europeans began colonizing the region in the 1600s, they too encountered the Apotamkin, though they renamed it the Gloucester Sea Serpent, for the town off of which it was most commonly seen.

These sightings were common through the 1800s, with a highpoint of 18 confirmed sightings in 1817. Occasionally the same serpent would even be seen by multiple observers from separate boats. At this time the seas off of New England were still teeming with fish, and the ocean still played an integral part in many peoples' lives. The abundance of food for the creature and the increasing number of human eyes on the water are the likely reasons for the fantastic number of sightings from this period.

These sightings were notable for their similarity. The serpent was almost universally described as between 60 and 100 feet long, roughly the diameter of a barrel, with a dark back above a lighter belly and a head similar to that of a horse. Many observers also make note of the animal's motion. It moved up and down "like a caterpiller," not side to side. As it swam, multiple humps could be seen as its back broke the surface of the water.

Gloucester Sea Serpent

Unfortunately, it has not been uncommon for the large animals of North America to suffer a decrease in numbers after the arrival of European colonists, and so it has been for the Gloucester Sea Serpent. From a peak in 1817, sightings became less and less common until they stopped altogether by the middle of the 20th century. The disappearance of the Gloucester Sea Serpent corresponds with the weakening and eventual collapse of the North Atlantic fish population. It is likely that overfishing removed an important food source for the sea serpents near Gloucester and they either migrated to more productive waters or went extinct.

Our second North American sea serpent is notable both for its contemporary nature and its similarity to the

Gloucester Sea Serpent. This creature is nearly identical to the species described in New England in both appearance and behavior, but lives across the continent, in another ocean, in the cold waters of the North Pacific.

Cadborosaurus willsi is the scientific name given to this beast by researchers Edward Bousfield and Paul LeBlond. The earliest sightings of "Caddy" are undocumented, but the creature was known to the First Nation Peoples of Canada. Caddy is found in Native imagery up and down the Pacific coast. One of the earliest documented sightings comes from a crew member on the fur-trading ship *Columbia* in 1791. Since then, there have been more than 300 sightings of *Cadborosaurus willsi*, most occurring off the coast of British Columbia, but some occurring as far south as San Francisco. Dozens of Caddy carcasses have washed ashore, most of which have been written off by skeptics as decomposed whales or sharks. There are also two accounts of juvenile *Cadborosaurus willsi* having been caught by fisherman, the first in 1968 and the second in 1991.

Cadborosaurus willsi is a serpentine animal reaching 70 feet in length. Witnesses describe it as having an equine-like head and hair or bristles along its neck. Propelled by both anterior and posterior flippers, the creature is able to swim rapidly while appearing to put forth no effort whatsoever. Caddy often swims along the surface of the water, leaving nearly no wake, with only a few undulating humps exposed. The description of Caddy matches that of the Gloucester Sea Serpent in nearly every regard.

One notable sighting comes to us from a construction crew working in Stinson Beach, a small town located about 30 minutes north of San Francisco. Five members of the crew reported seeing the creature on October 31st, 1983. The weather was clear and the day was notably free of fog, providing observers with a clear view of the animal. The creature swam along the coast for at least ten minutes before diving underwater. None of the observers had ever seen an animal remotely similar to the beast, despite all of them having lived their entire lives near the ocean. Just two years later, two brothers reported seeing a 60 foot serpent in the San Francisco Bay, chasing sea lions in the water. Reports from both sightings made note of the vertical undulations the creature made when it moved, ruling out misidentification of oarfish and sharks.

This author believes that *Cadborosaurus willsi* and the Gloucester Sea Serpent are the same species. It is likely that this creature has a distribution extending across the Acrtic and northern Pacific oceans, with a historical range extending south into the northern Atlantic ocean. With careful management expected to allow a rebound in the north Atlantic fisheries, it will be interesting to see if the Gloucester Sea Serpent returns to its historical range.

STELLER'S SEA APE

Georg Wilhelm Steller was a German polymath who took part in explorations of Kamchatka and Alaska in the 1740s. An avid botanist and zoologist, he was the first

European to describe many species of plants and animals found along the coast of the northern reaches of the Pacific. Ten of these organisms were named after Georg Steller. Some of them, like the Steller's jay and the Steller's sea lion, are still common sightings in western North America. Some, like the Steller's sea cow, have gone extinct. One species has not yet been recognized by the mainstream scientific community.

Steller recorded his sighting of a creature he named the Sea Ape on August 10th, 1741, while sailing off the Shumagin Islands in Alaska. Steller observed the animal raise its head out of the water to watch the boat, and noted its playful behavior. Steller described the animal as roughly five feet in length, with a body covered in thick gray fur and a lighter belly. The animal had a tail like that of a shark, with no discernable anterior appendages. The head of the beast was described as looking like that of a hog. Having never heard of any creature even remotely resembling what was before him, Steller was certain that he had discovered a new species.

Only one report of Steller's Sea Ape has been made in the nearly 300 years since the initial sighting. Miles Smeeton was sailing with his daughter and a friend near the Aleutian Islands in 1969 when an unknown animal was seen by the three of them. After returning to land they came across Steller's description of his Sea Ape, and all three agreed that it matched what they saw. It is worth noting that Smeeton, a veteran of the Second World War, was an experienced sailor and is regarded as a man of fine character. The lack of Sea Ape sightings may be attributed to the remote habitat of the creature and the social isolation of the few people who live there.

TRINITY ALPS GIANT SALAMANDER

Giant salamanders may sound like fiction, but they are very real. The largest salamander in the world is the Chinese giant salamander, which can grow up to six feet in length. Not far behind is the Japanese giant salamander at five feet. Giant salamanders can be found in North America as well. The hellbender is a salamander found in the streams of the Appalachian Mountains. Hellbenders have been known to reach two and a half feet in length. A similar creature is reported to live in the Trinity Alps of northern California, though no specimen has ever been preserved and it is not recognized by the mainstream scientific community.

Trinity Alps Giant Salamander

The first reports of the Trinity Alps Giant Salamander date to the mid 1800s, and sightings have been declining ever since. The giant salamanders of Asia and the hellbender have suffered severe population declines, and the same fate may have befallen the Trinity Alps Giant Salamander. Cryptozoologists searching for this creature should begin in any of the fast moving streams of the Trinity Alps Wilderness Area, northwest of Redding, California. Giant salamanders prefer well-aerated, fast-moving water and spend most of their time hiding under rocks, waiting for prey to float by. Hellbenders are most active around sunset, and the Trinity Alps Giant Salamander may share this trait.

WHITE RIVER MONSTER

The White River of Arkansas and Missouri is a short river, but it carries more water than many rivers twice its length. It is home to a mysterious creature known only as the White River Monster. Reports of the beast date back to the American Civil War, when a mysterious, unseen animal was blamed for overturning two Union boats. The first documented description is from 1915, when a farmer reported seeing a gray-skinned creature the length of three cars. Interest in the White River Monster peaked in 1937, when farmer Bramlett Bateman, fearing for his livestock, applied for a permit to blow up the creature with TNT. His permit was denied, but word got out and monster hunters from around the nation poured into Newport, Arkansas. More than 100 people encountered the creature that summer, though nobody was successful in killing it despite many trying with weapons ranging from spears and clubs to machine guns and dynamite. Interest in the monster rose again in 1971, when multiple people reported seeing a "boxcar sized" fish in the river. This particular frenzy caused the Arkansas State Legislature to create a White River Monster Refuge Area in 1973. It is illegal to harm the White River Monster within this designated stretch of the river.

Skeptics of the White River Monster claim that it is a case of mass hysteria, perhaps even a hoax perpetuated by Mr. Bateman that, through the powers of suggestion, caused others to believe they saw something that wasn't really there. Other skeptics believe that the sightings, while real, were simply sightings of an elephant seal that swam up the Mississippi River. While an elephant seal would fit many of the descriptions given, it is difficult to believe that such a creature may have found its way up the Mississippi. The closest populations of elephant seals are on the Pacific Coast of California. Seals traveling to the Mississippi River would have to swim all the way to the Panama Canal and then up the Atlantic. Furthermore, the sightings cover a timespan longer than the lifespan of an elephant seal, necessitating a breeding population of seals that established themselves in the Mississippi River and its tributaries. Occam's Razor suggests it is more likely that there is, in fact, an undiscovered species in the White River.

Terrestrial Cryptids

AHUITZOTL

The Ahuitzotl is a small, dog-like creature from central Mexico that lives near lakes and streams. The beast is covered in an oily black fur that repels water and gives the Ahuitzotl a smooth appearance everywhere but its back, where the hair stands on end. First described by the Aztecs, Ahuitzotl means "spiny water-loving thing," likely a reference to spiky hair on the creatures back. Despite having a name that refers to the Ahuitzotl as "water-loving," multiple reports confirm that the creature does live on land, though it is comfortable in the water and often hunts and feeds along shorelines. The paws of the Ahuitzotl are described as having the ability to grasp and are often compared to those of a raccoon. The tail is also said to have a hand on the end of it, though this may simply be a reference to its prehensile nature.[19] The Ahuitzotl has a reputation for drowning humans and eating the soft, fleshy parts. Caution should be exercised while in Ahuitzotl territory.

BEAVER EATER

The Yukon Territory is a wild place, almost completely untouched by human development. There are only 34,000 people in all of the Yukon, and nearly all of them live in the town of Whitehorse. If there is any place for a large mammal to live undiscovered, it is here. Though the Beaver Eater is most often seen by trappers and outdoor enthusiasts, the best description comes from an oil worker doing preliminary engineering for a proposed pipeline near Eagle Plains in 1997. He described the Beaver Eater as a mammal slightly smaller than a bear. It was covered with long, brown fur and walked slowly on all fours. The observer was a lifetime resident of the Yukon Territory and an avid hunter. He was

Beaver Eater

certain that the animal was one he had never seen before. This description, and others like it, have led experts to conclude that the Beaver Eater is likely some kind of ground sloth, perhaps a survivor of the Pleistocene extinction. The last ground sloths in North America are thought by the mainstream scientific community to have gone extinct shortly after the last ice age.[20] The creature derives its name from its habit of breaking open beaver lodges and eating the inhabitants. It is believed that the Beaver Eater only does this in the middle of winter, when food is scarce. The summertime diet of the Beaver Eater is uncertain.

CHUPACABRA

The Chupacabra is a relatively recent addition to the cryptid canon, with the first documented sighting occurring in 1995. That year saw a rash of livestock killings in eastern Puerto Rico. The animals were all found drained of blood and with three puncture wounds in their torsos. As news of the attacks spread, people came forward with reports of earlier occurrences. A particularly horrific outbreak of livestock killings that occurred in 1975 in the Puerto Rican town of Moca has since been attributed to the Chupacabra.

The name of the creature roughly translates to "goat-sucker." This descriptive and chilling moniker was coined by the Puerto Rican comedian Silverio Parez, and was quickly adopted by the general public. Sightings of the

Chupacabra have occurred outside of Puerto Rico, mostly in Central America, Mexico, and the Southwestern United States.

Chupacabra

Eyewitnesses to the attacks describe the creature as being roughly four feet long, with smooth or scaly skin, and a pronounced ridge of small spikes or coarse hair along the length of its spine. Many observers describe the Chupacabra as "reptilian." The Chupacabra is nocturnal, and the creature is not often seen directly, rather its presence is inferred from the dead and drained animal carcasses left in its wake. Coyotes, raccoons, and domestic dogs can, when infested with mange, look alarmingly similar to the Chupacabra. Care should be taken to avoid misidentification.

DEVIL MONKEY

These small, baboon-faced primates are commonly seen across southern North America, though rarely north of the Mason-Dixon Line. Most observers describe them as three to four feet tall, covered with shaggy gray fur, and possessing notably pointed ears. They are reported to move quickly and have the ability to jump fantastic distances. This jumping ability sometimes causes Devil Monkeys to be mistaken for escaped kangaroos or wallabies. Devil Monkeys are reported to be aggressive, especially if surprised, and utmost caution should be exercised in their presence.

The earliest reports of Devil Monkeys come from Appalachia in the 1930s. Sightings continued throughout the southeastern United States into the 1960s, when the bulk of the sightings shifted west to Texas, New Mexico and Arizona. It is speculated that increased human presence drove the Devil Monkeys out of the southeastern United States and into less populated areas. Since 2006 there have been an unusual number of sightings in Ohio and Illinois, perhaps due to the Devil Monkeys' range expanding north as a result of climate change.

Devil Monkey

ELMENDORF BEAST

The Elmendorf Beast is the name given to a creature shot by rancher David McAnally near Elmendorf, Texas in August, 2004. The carcass of the animal weighed 20 pounds, and was covered in a leathery, bluish-gray skin. The creature was tied to several livestock attacks in the area. The rash of attacks ended abruptly with the shooting of the beast.

Many people have speculated that the Elmendorf Beast is actually a Chupacabra, but the carcass differs from descriptions the Chupacabra in several regards. The Elmendorf beast is smaller than a Chupacabra, its skin is the wrong color, and it lacks the tell-tale row of spines on its back. Furthermore, the carcass was described as more canine than reptilian and none of the attacked livestock had the three puncture wounds common to victims of the Chupacabra. Local zoologists studied the carcass, and were unable to conclusively identify the animal.

FLATWOODS MONSTER

The Flatwoods Monster is a creature that is alleged to exist based on multiple sightings occurring on the same day in September of 1952. The sightings took place in rural Braxton County, West Virginia. While the monster is sometimes classified as a cryptid, it is more likely a close encounter with an extraterrestrial being. The encounter was preceded by a flash of light across the sky, and the being itself was accompanied by a mysterious red light, believed to be the craft that the being arrived in. Further evidence that the origin of the Flatwoods Monster is extraterrestrial can be found in the fact that the observers reported illness in the days following the encounter, a common occurrence in extraterrestrial encounters but a phenomenon undocumented in cryptid sightings.

GOAT PEOPLE

Stories of creatures described as half-man and half-goat are fairly common in the eastern United States. Three of the most famous are the Pope-lick Monster, from Kentucky; the Lake Worth Monster, from Texas; and the Maryland Goatman, from, obviously, Maryland. These creatures are usually described as having the legs and sometimes head of a goat, but the body of a man. Stories about Goat People often include strange and macabre origin legends. Common themes are that the Goat People were escaped genetic experiments or circus sideshows, or that they are the results of unholy relations with the devil. The Goat People seem less interested in staying hidden and more interested in terrorizing humans who seek them out. They often carry a bloody axe or some other weapon. Occasionally they are known to attack amorous teenagers who have parked their cars in remote locations.

It is the opinion of the author that Goat People are not true cryptids, but merely legends. While it is possible that there may be a species of animal with both ovine and ape-like characteristics, and that sightings of these animals has given rise to legends of goat-people, satyrs, and fauns alike, the Goat People of the eastern United States do not fit into this category. Most reports read like cliched horror stories. True cryptids are animals that have managed to stay hidden and undiscovered. While they are sometimes misunderstood and their actions construed as malevolent, the idea that a cryptid would carry a weapon or punish sinful teenagers is ridiculous.

Maryland Goatman

HODAG

The Hodag is a cryptid that roams the deep woods of northern Wisconsin. The first sighting was reported in 1893 outside the small town of Rhinelander. Newspaper articles from the time describe it as a chimera, with body parts resembling bits of frogs, elephants, dinosaurs, and bears. These vague and outlandish descriptions gathered national attention in the 1890s. Taking advantage of the press was Rhinelander businessman Eugene Shepard, who organized a fake photo shoot with a Hodag carcass and even displayed a "live" Hodag as part of a sideshow act. Hoaxes aside, credible accounts of encounters with Hodags continued to surface.[21]

A more sober description of the creature comes to us from a 1967 sighting. Joseph Kurzman and his son William were hunting for deer on their family's hunting land near Tomahawk Lake, roughly 10 miles northwest of Rhinelander. They had set up an elevated deer stand on the edge of a small pasture, but hadn't seen a deer all day. Just as they were about to give up and head home for the day they saw a small animal emerge from the forest. They initially identified it as a wolverine, but revised their opinion upon closer inspection through the scopes on their rifles. Although the general size, shape, and color were right, this animal was stockier than a wolverine and its head was larger and lacking any sort of a snout. There was also a very well defined ridge of what the Kurzmans described as "porcupine quills" along the animals back and tail. William apparently wanted to shoot the creature, but his father stopped him, claiming he was uncomfortable shooting something he couldn't identify.

JACKALOPE

Like the fur-bearing trout, examples of Jackalopes appear in gift shops across Western North America. These souvenirs are nothing more than taxidermied Frankenstein's Monsters. They are simply rabbits with deer antlers attached, and no cryptozoologist worth their binoculars would ever be fooled by them.

Jackalope

Occasionally, a photo or a story will surface about a rabbit with horns being seen in the wild. The horns on these animals look nothing like the antlers found on the gift shop Jackalopes, a fact which lends the stories a certain credibility. These "horns" are dark brown and rough. There are often more than two of them and they don't always grow out of the top of the rabbit's head.

They often grow down from the jaw, or out of the animals mouth.

These sightings have an explanation that is firmly outside the realm of cryptozoology. These unfortunate leporids are simply jackrabbits that have been infected by the Cottontail Rabbit Papillomavirus.[22] This virus causes a cancer that manifests itself through large, grotesque, cranial tumors. These tumors give the rabbit a startling, demonic appearance and are almost certainly the source of the mythical Jackalope.

LIZARD MAN OF SCAPE ORE SWAMP

The Lizard Man of Scape Ore Swamp is a seven-foot-tall, bi-pedal hominid that lives in the swamps and sewers of Lee County, South Carolina. Sightings of Lizard Men are nothing new; they are documented in artifacts from ancient Greece, Egypt, and China, but the Lizard Man of Scape Ore Swamp managed to remain in seclusion until it was seen by a South Carolina teenager in 1988.

Christopher Davis was returning from work at two in the morning on June 29th, 1988, when his car's tire went flat. He stopped to change it, and, as he was finishing up, he heard a thumping sound behind him. Looking over his shoulder, he saw a tall, green creature with glowing red eyes running toward him. Christopher quickly got into his car and locked the door. The creature then attacked the car, completely destroying the side mirror and scratching the roof. Christopher escaped and made a report to the police, in which he described the animal as having "three big fingers, long black nails, and green rough skin." Further sightings were reported to the Lee County Sheriff's office through the fall of 1988. Sightings have tapered off since then, but still occur occasionally.

No one knows what caused the Lizard Man of Scape Ore Swamp to leave the waters where it had lived, undisturbed, for so long. Some people speculate that encroaching development in Lee County altered the creature's behavior. Others believe that environmental degradation affected its food supply and forced it out of the swamp in search of sustenance. Anyone attempting to find the Lizard Man of Scape Ore Swamp should exercise extreme caution as the creature has demonstrated incredible strength and aggressive behavior.

LOVELAND FROG

The Loveland Frog is a humanoid, possibly amphibious creature found near the Little Miami River in southwest Ohio. The creature is also sometimes referred to as "The Frogman of the Little Miami River."

The first report that definitively points to the Loveland Frog is from 1955, although ancient legends from the local native people may reference a similar creature. The creature is described as being three to four feet long, with muted, smooth skin. The color of the creature's skin is usually reported as greenish-brown, though it has also been called gray or reddish-brown. These discrepancies may be due to the fact that the Loveland Frog is most commonly encountered in the low-light early morning hours, when colors can be hard to distinguish. It is often seen crouching like a frog, then rising onto its long and muscular hind legs before running away. Its face has been described as frog-like, iguana-like, or reptilian.

Loveland Frog

The most credible sightings of the Loveland Frog are a pair of encounters from 1972. These sightings are noteworthy because they were both made by Loveland

Police Officers and both are recorded in official police reports. The first officer to see the Loveland Frog was Ray Shockey. Officer Shockey was on patrol along the Little Miami River early in the morning on March 3, 1972. He was driving slowly due to the icy conditions, and was forced to stop abruptly when an animal scurried across Riverside Drive in front of him. Shockey searched the ditch with his spotlight and illuminated a crouched creature matching the description of the Loveland Frog. The animal quickly rose onto its hind legs and ran off.

The second sighting by a Loveland Police Officer occurred not long after, on March 17th of the same year. Officer Mark Matthews was also on early morning patrol near the river when he stopped to remove an apparently dead animal from the side of the road. Upon exiting his patrol car, the animal rose into a crouch and turned toward officer Matthews. As Matthews was unholstering his gun, the animal rose and ran off.

MACFARLANE'S BEAR

The existence of MacFarlane's Bear is postulated from a single specimen shot by Inuit hunters in 1864. The Inuits of northern Canada were familiar with both grizzly bears and polar bears, but they had never seen a bear like this. It was enormous, and its fur was an unusual yellow color. The hunters gave the skull and the hide to a naturalist named Roderick MacFarlane, who in turn shipped the samples to the Smithsonian Institution in Washington,

MacFarlane's Bear

D.C. The skull and hide remained in storage for fifty years until being rediscovered and declared a new species of bear. References to animals matching MacFarlane's bear have been found in the journal entries of fur-traders, with the frequency of such entries declining from a peak in the 1880s. Scientists believe that the bear may have been a holdover from the Pleistocene Era, and may now be extinct.

MELON HEADS

Sightings of Melon Heads, sometimes known as "Wobble-heads," are relatively common across the Midwestern and Northeastern United States. People who have seen the creatures describe them as small hominids, only three to four feet tall, with disproportionately large heads, sunken eyes, and skin so pale as to sometimes appear translucent. Sightings are most frequent along the western edge of the Appalachian Mountains. They seem to prefer to live in the deepest, most remote portions of the forest. Anyone searching for Melon Heads should start by driving through and hiking near the small towns of northern Kentucky, western West Virginia, and extreme southwest Ohio. Most sightings come from sportsmen and people who make a living in the woods, such as miners and loggers. While attacks by Melon Heads are extremely rare, people who live near them are afraid of the creatures and attempt to give them a wide berth. In south-eastern Ohio the Melon Heads are believed to possess psychic powers. Witnesses are often shaken by their encounters with these creatures and thus unwilling to talk openly about them. Local bars and pubs may offer the best opportunities to glean tips from besotted locals.

MENEHUNE

Deep in the inland forests of Hawaii, far from the tourist filled beaches, live the Menehune. The Menehune are a species of tiny people, looking much like humans, but only a few feet tall. The Menehune subsist on a diet of bananas and fish, and are known to be skilled builders. Among the structures built by the Menehune are stone lined irrigation canals, fish ponds for aquaculture, and small temples and shrines on Necker Island.[23] The Menehune are extremely difficult to find, and some

Hawaiians believe that they have magical powers that aid their ability to hide. The Menehune are not believed to be related to the above mentioned Melon Heads.

MICHIGAN DOGMAN

The Michigan Dogman is a human-canine chimera named for the state in which it is most often encountered. The Dogman has the body of a human and walks on two legs, but has the head of a wolf. It is sometimes asserted that the body of the creature is covered in fur or that the hands also show canine features, but these traits are not common to all reports. The Dogman is often seen living in packs of wolves, where it is presumed to occupy the alpha position.

The first documented sighting of the Dogman occurred in Michigan in 1887. The woods of northern Michigan were under extensive logging at the time, and it was two lumberjacks working in Wexford County who made the terrifying discovery. The two men were walking through the woods when they encountered what they thought was a feral dog. They decided to follow the animal, presumably due to a lack of entertainment. The dog ran inside a hollow log, and when the men tried to coax it out a six foot tall man with the head of a wolf emerged instead. The men fled. I do not believe that the "feral dog" the men were chasing turned into the Dogman, rather that the Dogman was already inside the log and emerged to defend a member of its pack.

Reports of the Dogman surfaced often in the years that followed. In 1897 a farmer was found dead at his plow, the nearby ground covered in strange tracks. In early 1903 a widow reported that a pack of wolves that walk like men circled her home every night. In 1911 a sheriff filed a report concerning four mysteriously dead horses,

Michigan Dogman

again the ground was covered in strange tracks. A ship captain shot a wild dog that attacked him from its hind legs in 1937. A priest saw strange scratches at the door of a church in 1939. And in 1950, two fishermen encountered the creature on the shore of Lake Michigan and fought it off with their oars.

While the slow steady trickle of sightings made the creature famous across the Midwest, the Dogman finally achieved national renown in 1987 when a radio disc-jockey in Traverse City recorded a spoof song about the legend. The song became a surprise hit, and over 100 people called in to the station to tell of their own encounters with the creature.

While the Dogman is most commonly associated with northern Michigan, it is not unusual to encounter it elsewhere. In nearby Wisconsin, the animal has been known as the Beast of Bray Road since the 1930s, when it was renamed for the location of a famous sighting that occurred in the southeast portion of the state, on a quiet country lane near the town of Elkhorn. Reports of the Beast of Bray Road peaked in the 1970s and 80s, a time when many people were coming forth with accounts of sightings they had previously kept suppressed.

The animal is often initially mistaken for either a wolf or a bear, understandably, as the creature is covered in a grayish-brown fur. Closer examination of the animal's head rules out the bear identification, as the creature's snout, face, and ears are universally described as canine.

The beast is commonly reported to be seven feet in length, longer than the gray wolf of nearby Minnesota. The Beast of Bray Road and the Michigan Dogman are often seen standing on their hind legs, a behavior that does not commonly occur in wolves. A sense of the animal's intelligence and vaguely defined "human-like features" are often also reported. Many observers also report that the eyes of the beast reflect light particularly well, and appear to glow yellow.

There is also a long history of Dogman sightings in Minnesota, but two recent sightings are particularly noteworthy. The first took place north of Duluth, at an Air National Guard Facility in 1999. The observer, a member of the 148th Fighter Wing, was on patrol when he encountered a large wolf-like creature standing on its hind legs. The encounter was brief, as the creature quickly ran into the woods. The observer was a trained member of the military and an experienced woodsman.

The second notable sighting took place outside of Fergus Falls in the spring of 2006. The encounter is remarkable because the creature was seen in broad daylight. The observer, an avid hunter and outdoor enthusiast, was driving along a gravel country road when he spotted what looked like a large wolf stalking deer from its hind legs. The observer also noted that the hands looked long and slender with opposable thumbs.

It is worth noting the vastness of the region known as the Northwoods. This massive boreal forest covers half of Canada and stretches across the upper United States from Montana to Maine. It is very possible that an undiscovered species of mammal could remain hidden in this sparsely populated region. Most of the Dogman sightings in Michigan, Wisconsin, and Minnesota have occured within or very close to the Northwoods.

Some cryptozoologists believe that Dogmen are actually a surviving population of dire wolf, a species thought to have gone extinct only 10,000 years ago. Common during the most recent ice age, this animal's range overlapped with that of the Dogman.[25] The dire wolf was larger than the wolves of today, but not as large as the Dogman is reported to be. It is possible, however, that over 10,000 years of undocumented evolution the dire wolf has increased in size.

MONTAUK MONSTER

In July of 2008 a mysterious carcass washed ashore near the northern tip of Long Island. Local residents and summer beachgoers alike were unable to identify the creature, which was soon dubbed the Montauk Monster. The decaying carcass was the size of a large cat. It was in rough condition, with bits of fur still present along its back and bones exposed where fish and birds had nibbled on it. The animal appeared to have walked on all fours, but the legs of the creature were longer in proportion to its body than those of most quadrupeds. A long, skinny tail hung from the animal's rear end. The head and face of the creature were perhaps the most bizarre. While the skull structure suggested that of a sheep, the snout ended in what appeared to be a menacing, toothed beak. The carcass was discovered by vacationers at Ditch Plains Beach, a popular location for surfing. It was seen by an unknown number of people, and multiple photos were taken. By the time these photos reached the news media, the carcass had been removed by an unknown person or persons. The photos were scrutinized by zoologists around the world who were unable to reach a consensus on the identification of the animal.[24]

One hypothesis is that the animal is not actually a cryptid, but some sort of escaped experiment from the nearby Plum Island Animal Disease Center, located across Gardiner's Bay, a short 15 miles from where the carcass washed ashore. Reports from July 2008 claim that representatives from Plum Island were present in Montauk and were attempting to discover the fate of the carcass. This secretive federal research facility was started in 1954 with the stated intent of studying and preventing diseases in livestock, but was quickly turned into a center for biological weapons research. The center has been linked, though not definitively, to outbreaks of Lyme Disease, West Nile Disease and Dutch Duck Plague.[26] If the Montauk Monster was indeed an escapee from Plum Island, the inevitable government coverup would explain the rapid and unusual disappearance of the carcass. Government conspiracy websites may be helpful in further researching the Montauk Monster.

OZARK HOWLER

The Ozark Howler is a cryptid found in the Ozark Mountains of Arkansas, Oklahoma, and Missouri. Many observers of the Ozark Howler initially mistake it for a black bear, as it is roughly the same size and color. The fur of the Ozark Howler is shaggier than that of the

Ozark Howler

Black Bear, but the most distinguishing difference is that the Ozark Howler has a pair of horns on its head. Some accounts describe the horns as "smooth, and on the sides of the head, like a buffalo," while others describe them as "long, like an antelope." The discrepancy in horn descriptions is likely due to the fact that most Ozark Howlers are encountered in the deep woods and at sunrise or sunset, in low-light conditions.

It is recommended that cryptozoologists seeking the Ozark Howler begin their search in the Upper Buffalo Wilderness. This federally designated wilderness area has been uninhabited since 1948 and is in the center of Howler country. A permit is required for camping in the wilderness area, and backcountry skills are required. Provisions can be bought in either Little Rock, roughly 100 miles southeast, or Fayetteville, roughly 100 miles to the northwest. Note that the Ozark Howler is considered dangerous, and extreme caution should be exercised in the event of an encounter.

PHANTOM CATS

Some cryptids are animals not yet known to science, and others are animals known but believed to be extinct. Phantom Cats are a third type: known, extant animals seen so far out of their accepted range that the reports are dismissed by both mainstream scientists and the popular media. The two largest cats in North America are the cougar and the jaguar, and it is believed that most of the sightings of Phantom Cats in North America are one of these two species.

Jaguar

Cougars, also known as mountain lions, are the most common large cat in North America. While they once roamed the entire continent with the exception of the far northern reaches of Canada and Alaska, their contemporary range is much smaller. Scientists now believe that they can only be found in Central America, Mexico, the western United States and Canada. There is also a very small population living in the extreme southern tip of Florida. Reports of cougars outside of their scientifically accepted range are not uncommon. They have been shot and killed in Minnesota, Michigan, and within the city limits of Chicago. Credible sightings have occurred as far east as suburban New York City. It is not unusual for males to wander thousands of miles outside their territory when unable to find a mate. When investigating Phantom Cat sightings, the cougar should be the initial suspect.

Jaguars also once ranged over much of North America, from Central America to the extreme southwest portion of the United States. They can now only be reliably found in Central America and pockets of Mexico. The cats do make trips into the southern United States, however, and have been documented by mounted trail cameras.[27] The jaguar is larger than the cougar and is usually spotted, although it can sometimes appear nearly all black. It is the second most likely explanation for a Phantom Cat sighting.

Occasionally a witness to a Phantom Cat will insist that they saw a lion or a tiger. These are easily identifiable cats and anyone claiming to have seen one should be taken seriously. There are more tigers held in captivity in the United States than there are remaining in the wild. Most of these are held by private individuals, and not always with the full blessing of the law. Escaped big cats can be surprisingly difficult to find and news of the escape is often supressed by owners who were not supposed to be in possession of a big cat in the first place.

PUKWUDGIE

The Pukwudgies are small hominids that live near Cape Cod. Standing only two or three feet tall, they look similar to humans, but have exaggerated features and smooth gray skin. The earliest reports of Pukwudgies are part of Wampanoag folklore. The creatures are said to have magical powers. Most cryptozoologists consider Pukwudgies mythical creatures, and not true cryptids. Despite this skepticism, Pukwudgie sightings are common in rural Massachusetts and strange events are still commonly attributed to them.

ROUGAROU

The Rougarou is a Dogman that inhabits the swamps of southern Louisiana. The creature draws its name from the French word for werewolf: loup-garou. Beliefs concerning the Rougarou are diverse, and many local legends are colored by traditional European werewolf mythology. It is this author's belief that the Rougarou is simply a population of Dogman closely related to the Michigan Dogan and the Beast of Bray Road.

SASQUATCH

The Sasquatch, also known as Bigfoot, is perhaps the most famous cryptid in all of North America. As the largest nonhuman ape native to the continent, Sasquatch is unmistakable. It walks on its hind legs and is between six and nine feet tall. The creature's shoulders and waist are wider than those of a human, and the body is bulkier overall. The Sasquatch is covered in medium length fur or hair, usually a dark brown but sometimes closer to black or to red. The arms are longer in proportion to its height than those of a human, and the Sasquatch hangs them low as it walks with hunched shoulders and a

Sasquatch

distinctive bent-knee gait. Often seen eating fish or clams, Sasquatch is also reported to eat berries and other plants. Observers often notice a pungent, body-odor type smell. Sasquach is thought to be predominantly nocturnal.

The image of the Sasquatch is known worldwide. It is used to market music festivals, to sell beef jerky, pizza, and skateboards. Sasquatch has been the star of television shows and Hollywood movies. There is even a Monster Truck named after the beast. But the most exciting thing about Sasquatch is that there have been literally thousands of documented sightings, the earliest of which come from the native people of the Pacific Northwest.

Nearly half of all Sasquatch sightings occur in British Colombia, Washington, Oregon, and California. This is also the area where most of the native stories concerning the Sasquatch come from. To many of these tribes, the Sasquatch is not a cryptid, but an accepted animal. To others, the Sasquatch takes on more mystical or supernatural powers. Some tribes consider the Sasquatch to be kind and gentle creatures of the mountains, while to others they are malevolent beasts, harming and sometimes kidnapping people who stumble across them.

One particularly notable Sasquatch report comes to us from none other than the 26th President of the United States, Theodore Roosevelt. In 1889 Roosevelt published *The Wilderness Hunter*, an account of his years spent living and hunting along the American frontier. In this book he recalls a tale told to him by an old trapper who experienced a Sasquatch encounter in Idaho sometime in the 1850s. There are many more reports of encounters from hunters and trappers throughout the late 1800s. Most of these paint the Sasquatch to be a dangerous and aggressive creature. This directly contradicts many contemporary accounts that describe the Sasquatch as shy and elusive, much preferring hiding from human contact to fighting. It is possible that the hunters and trappers exaggerated the ferocity of the Sasquatch in an attempt to make themselves appear more heroic, or to make the West seem more wild and dangerous. Alternatively, Sasquatch behavior could have become more subdued as they encountered and learned about the power and danger of firearms.

Reports of Sasquatch sightings have not slowed down with time, instead, they have increased as more and more people move into Sasquatch habitat. There have been Sasquatch sightings in nearly every state, though the number and reliability of such sightings rapidly decrease as you move east of the Rocky Mountains. There are numerous websites that document Sasquatch sightings and many cryptozoologists have made collecting these reports their life's work. There has been more evidence connected to Sasquatch than to nearly any other cryptid. Photographs, videos, footprint casts, bits of fur, and droppings have all been collected at one time or another.

The most famous video or photo of a Sasquatch is undoubtedly the Patterson-Gimlin film from 1967. Shot on the Bluff Creek, in the extreme northwest corner of

California, the film shows a female Sasquatch calmly walking along a riverbed and looking over her shoulder at the pair of filmmakers. This has become the single most iconic Sasquatch image. The Patterson-Gimlin film is important because it clearly captures details common to many Sasquatch sightings. The creature's arms droop and its back is hunched as it ambles along with a gait that is distinctly non-human. The skull of the creature shows a distinct sagittal crest. And the breasts of the Sasquatch are covered in fur, a feature not found on any other ape.

Sasquatch footprints are a common finding, and many have been preserved with plaster casts. Interestingly, all of the casts show a mid-foot pressure ridge, indicating that instead of flexing directly behind the toes as a human foot does, Sasquatch feet flex farther back. The universality of this feature is strong evidence for the authenticity of the footprint casts. The unusual flex point of the foot is also consistent with the unusual gait shown in videos of the Sasquatch.

Cryptozoologists have been fortunate enough to collect numerous samples of Sasquatch DNA. Often, this is in the form of hair found attached to trees, shrubs or fences. Unfortunately, collected Sasquatch DNA often goes untested, as most people do not have the means or the knowledge to test and analyze the samples. One researcher, Dr. Melba S. Ketchum, has attemped to solve this problem by collecting and analyzing over 100 Sasquatch DNA samples submitted to her by helpful cryptozoologists. She determined that the contemporary

Sasquatch is likely the result of humans breeding with an unknown ape species roughly 15,000 years ago.[28] Dr. Ketchum has submitted her results to peer-reviewed journals as is standard scientific procedure. The mainstream scientific community has been reluctant to work with Dr. Ketchum, but her paper is available online for anyone to read and analyze.

Not all Sasquatch sightings occur in the Pacific Northwest. Many animals have historical ranges vastly larger than their contemporary ranges, and it may also be so with Sasquatch. Reports of large, upright apes were common in the southeastern United States until the 1970s. Most of these sightings were in the swamps of Florida, though some were as far west as Arkansas and as far north as North Carolina. Named the "Skunk Ape" due to the unpleasant smell that often accompanied it, this creature was likely a subspecies of Sasquatch. Alas, it seems to have gone the way of the Florida panther, suffering a dramatic drop in population. Skunk Apes are now only rarely seen. While the bulk of the Sasquatch population appears to live west of the Rocky Mountians, sightings are not uncommon in the northern woods that stretch across southern Canada and the northern United States. Many other regions have their own names for the Sasquatch. In Texas they call it "The Wild Man of the Navidad." In Ohio it is "The Grassman." It is hoped that genetic testing will reveal whether these individuals are lone survivors of dwindling subpopulations, or if they are individual wandering Sasquatch from the Pacific Northwest.

SEWER ALLIGATOR

Alligators are known to inhabit sewers and drainpipes in their natural range, but reports also occasionally surface of alligators in the sewers of northern cities, particularly New York City. It is believed that these Sewer Alligators originated as pets, with their owners either flushing them down the toilet or placing them in storm drains when the gators grow too large to be comfortably kept. Enough people have done this to create a stable, breeding population of Sewer Alligators. Steam pipes for Manhattan's massive heating system keep the sewers warm enough through the winter for the cold-blooded reptiles to survive, and the abundance of rats and other rodents provides ample food.

Sewer Alligator

The most detailed and credible account of the alligators in New York's sewers comes from Robert Daley's 1959 book, *The World Beneath the City*. The book chronicles the challenges encountered in supplying the densely populated island of Manhattan with the utilities needed for a modern city to thrive. For the book, Daley interviewed Teddy May, the former Commissioner of Sewers for New York City. May states that sewer inspectors first began reporting alligator encounters in 1935. May began an eradication campaign that involved poisoning the alligators and hunting down any survivors with rifles. The campaign was believed to be a success, but reports of Sewer Alligators again began surfacing in the 1960s and continue to this day.

SHEEPSQUATCH

Hailing from Point Pleasant, West Virginia, home of the Mothman, Sheepsquatch is a fairly controversial cryptid. Witnesses describe Sheepsquatch as a six or seven foot tall bipedal animal with the body of an ape and the head of a ram. The body is covered in shaggy white fur. Sheepsquatch is considered very shy, and encounters are brief as the animal is quick to hide from view. The fact that Sheepsquatch sightings were not reported until the 1990s along with the playful name have led some cryptozoologists to take a very negative view of the cryptid. They believe that the creature is an obvious fabrication and cheapens the entire field of research. Believers explain the recent appearance of Sheepsquatch by noting the similarities to the more common Goat People of the eastern United States. They claim that Sheepsquatch is simply a modern name for a creature that has been known for centuries.

SHUNKA WARAK'IN

The Shunka Warak'in is a dog or hyena-like cryptid native to the vast prairies of North America. The creature's name means "carries off dogs" in the language of the Ioway tribe. Commonly seen by Native Americans before European contact, habitat loss severely reduced the number of Shunka Warak'in and sightings had become increasingly rare by the end of the nineteenth century. Shunka Warak'in sightings are now extremely rare, as the tallgrass prairie it calls home has been almost completely tilled under. Note that in the Northwest Territories of Canada, the Shunka Warak'in is known by the name "Waheela."

While comparable in size to a wolf or a large dog, the Shunka Warak'in is identifiable by high shoulders that slope down to its head. In this way the body shape is more akin to that of a hyena than a wolf. The Shunka Wark'in is predominantly gray, but its coloration can have distinct red and yellow aspects. The Shunka Warak'in has been reported to occasionally scavenge dead carcasses. This behavior, in addition to its appearance, has led to considerable debate over the relationship of the Shunka Warak'in to other animals. Some believe it is a member of the canine family, while others believe it is likely related to the hyena, which is actually more closely related to the felines than the canines.

Incredibly, two known Shunka Warak'in have been killed. The first was an individual shot by Israel Ammon Hutchins in 1886 in southwest Montana, not far from Yellowstone National Park. The animal was mounted and is currently on display at a museum in Ennis, Montana. The second was shot in eastern Montana in November of 2006. The animal was responsible for the slaughter of over 120 sheep over a one year period. Initially, the kills were credited to wolves, and ranchers were given permits to shoot any wolves seen attacking their flocks. When the responsible creature was finally shot, however, it became clear that the animal was not a wolf. Unable to identify it, wildlife officials sent tissue samples to UCLA for analysis. Results were never released to the public.

TEXARKANA MUD DRAGON

The Texarkana Mud Dragon is a rarely seen cryptid from the banks of the Red River in southwest Arkansas and northwest Louisiana. Presumed to be an extremely large cicada, the Mud Dragon spends most of its life burrowed deep in the muddy river bank, emerging only once every 15 years to breed. Observers describe the Mud Dragon as a large, six to eight-inch-long, black insect with prominent, shiny eyes on the sides of its head. The wings of the Mud Dragon are proportionally shorter than those of the more common cicadas, extending only to the end of the body. There are no reports of Mud Dragons flying, and it is suspected that the wings are vestigial.

Mud Dragons have acquired a unique adaptation to help them avoid predators. Upon hatching from their eggs, Mud Dragon nymphs burrow deep into the muddy river bank. It is not known how deep Mud Dragons burrow, but other, smaller cicadas have been found eight feet beneath the surface. Here they wait and grow, surviving on fluids sucked from tree roots, until it is time to emerge 15 years later. After emerging, the adult Mud Dragons quickly breed and the females lay their eggs before dying. The 15 year waiting period prevents

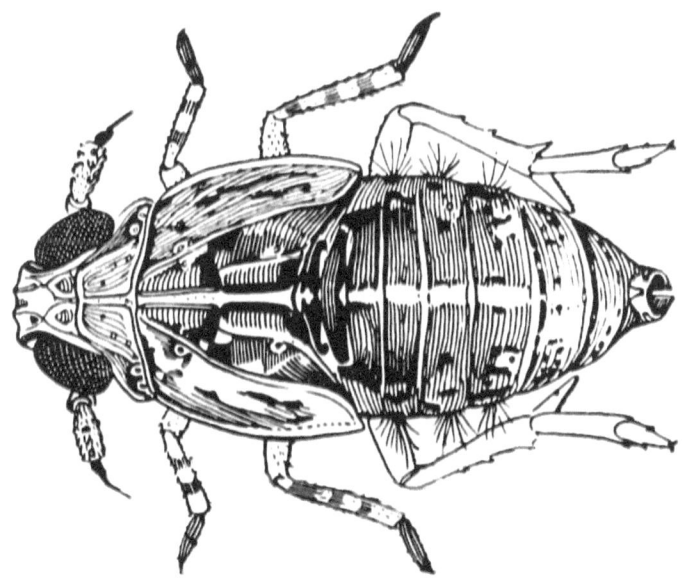

Texarkana Mud Dragon

predators from adopting a Mud Dragon specific diet, as they cannot count on a yearly emergence of prey. Other species of cicada have adopted similar techniques, with some species emerging in 17 and 13 year cycles.

Mud Dragons emergences have been reported in 2013, 1998, 1983, 1953, 1938, and 1893. It is assumed that they emerge every 15 years, with the gaps in the record being the result of unobserved emergences due to the low population and limited range of the species.[29] People digging for Mud Dragons in non-emergence years should look for clusters of four inch tall mud cones in otherwise smooth riverbank as evidence of Mud Dragon burrows.

Aerial Cryptids

CHICKCHARNEY

The Chickcharney is a cryptid found in the pine forests of Andros Island, the largest island in the Bahamas. The creature resembles a three-foot-tall barn owl, and is said to give good luck to people who treat it well. It is likely that Chickcharney sightings are, in fact, sightings of *Tyto pollens*, a flightless barn owl native to Andros Island that has been considered extinct by mainstream science since the 16th century.[30] *Tyto pollens* was common on Andros Island until European colonists harvested nearly all of the native forest. The forests surrounding the wetlands in the western portion of Andros Island were inaccessible to logging crews and were thus the only portion of the native forest saved from destruction. A small population of *Tyto pollens* likely survived here and was forgotten by the island's inhabitants. Reports of sightings from the most inaccessable portions of the forest must have spread through the Bahamas, and slowly, over time, morphed into the legend of the Chickcharney.

Chickcharney

FLYING ROD

Cryptids are by their nature elusive and hard to see, but Flying Rods take this to a new level. Flying Rods, also known as "Skyfish" or "Air Rods," are invisible to the naked eye, appearing only on film as elongated, worm-like creatures. Most people consider Flying Rods to be artifacts of insects moving across a camera's frame while the film is being exposed. Some people, however, are convinced that Flying Rods are a yet undescribed aerial species.

IVORY-BILLED WOODPECKER

The genus *Campephilus* contains the two largest woodpeckers in the world. The second largest woodpecker is *Campephilus principalus*, the Ivory-Billed Woodpecker. This bird is native to the southeastern United States and is considered extinct. The largest woodpecker on Earth is *Campephilus imperialis*, the Imperial Woodpecker, also known as the Mexican Ivorybill. This bird once ranged over most of Mexico, but sadly, it too is now considered extinct. Sightings of these birds still occur, leading many to believe that the mainstream scientific community is wrong about the extinction of the Ivory-Billed and the Imperial Woodpecker.[31] This could be a lucrative animal for a cryptozoologist to find, as one conservation group has offered $50,000.00 to anyone who can lead an ornithologist to a live Ivory-Billed Woodpecker.

Ivory-Billed Woodpecker

The Ivory-Billed Woodpecker of the United States is 20-21 inches long with a wingspan of 30 inches, about the size of a crow. The Imperial Woodpecker of Mexico is just slightly larger. Both birds have a dark blue or black body with white markings, a crested head, and a long, narrow, light-colored beak. Male birds of both species have a red crest, while the crest on females matches the body color. Ivory-Billed Woodpeckers inhabit hardwood swamps and old-growth pine forests. Imperial Woodpeckers prefer high-elevation pine forests. Both species are similar in appearance to the pileated woodpecker, though the pileated is smaller and has a much larger distribution. Anyone searching for the Ivory-Billed Woodpecker should familiarize themselves with the pileated woodpecker to avoid potentially embarrassing misidentifications.

JERSEY DEVIL

Wedged between and just south of the sprawling metropolises of New York City and Philadelphia are the New Jersey Pine Barrens, an expanse of pine forest that remains sparsely inhabited. The Pine Barrens are home to the Jersey Devil, a legendary winged goat. According to legend, the Jersey Devil is the 13th child of Mother Leeds, an area witch reported to have had relations with the Devil. While this tale of supernatural creation is almost certainly apocryphal, the beast has been seen by many reputable persons, including Joseph Bonaparte, brother of the French Emperor. The Jersey Devil is usually described as looking like a goat with leathery wings. The head of the beast is sometimes called "horse-like" instead of "goat-like," though tracks found in the Pine Barrens indicate that the Jersey Devil has cloven hooves, not solid hooves like horses. The creature is often seen to rear up on its hind legs before taking flight. The front legs are sometimes described as having claws, although this detail is not present in all accounts and may be the result of frightened witnesses ascribing monstrous traits to the Jersey Devil in their state of terror.

LONE PINE MOUNTAIN DEVIL

The Lone Pine Mountain Devil is a species of small, flying creatures inhabiting the Alabama Hills in east-central California. The creatures take their name from the nearby town of Lone Pine. Mountain Devils are the size

Lone Pine Mountain Devil

of large bats, and like bats they have leathery wings and hairy bodies. Unlike bats, the Devils have two sets of wings and a long, feathery tail. The first reports of the Devils come from early gold miners, who, struggling to survive in the harsh Mountain West, used the creatures as a source of food. Hunting pressure reduced the population drastically by 1900, and today the Devils are extremely rare.

MOTHMAN

Tales of the Mothman originate from the area around Point Pleasant, West Virginia. The first people to see the Mothman were a group of gravediggers in Clendenin, West Virginia. On November 12th, 1966, the men witnessed a winged human figure flying low over their heads. Three days later, two couples filed a police report describing a flying human with eyes that reflected red in their car's headlights. Similar descriptions surfaced over the course of the next year. On December 15, 1967, the Silver Bridge collapsed into the Ohio River, killing 46 people. No sightings of the Mothman have been reported since then, leading some to believe that the appearance of the Mothman was a portent of doom.

The lack of historical sightings, the sudden end to sightings, and the supernatural predictive abilities attributed to the Mothman have led most cryptozoologists to classify the Mothman as a "monster" and not a true cryptid. There are still people, however, that continue to search for the creature. There is also a small but adamant contingent of cryptozoologists that believe the Mothman sightings were actually a large, misidentified or yet undiscovered bird.

THUNDERBIRD

Common to many tribes from the Pacific Ocean to the Great Lakes, the Thunderbird is an important part of Native legend. These massive birds were credited with the ability to create storms and winds with their powerful wingbeats. While mainstream science considers the Thunderbird to be a supernatural myth, human encounters with these majestic creatures still occur to this day. There is also evidence that the stories of Thunderbirds leaving storms in their wake as they soar above the landscape may have their origins in the bird's habit of using the updrafts from weather fronts to keep its massive bulk aloft.

While stories of colossal birds have been told for as long as humans have inhabited North America, the first documented encounter was in April of 1890. Two cowboys in the Arizona Territory shot and killed a bird larger than any they had seen before. They hauled the creature back to town, where it created quite a stir. A photograph was taken with the animal's wings stretched out to nearly the length of a barn. The photograph was published in the Tombstone Epitaph, though, sadly, no copies have survived. This particular creature was said to have leathery wings like a bat and a head like an alligator. The description does not match those from later encounters, and may have been an embellishment intended to sell papers, considering that journalistic integrity was not a hallmark of the Old West.

Thunderbird

Most of the more recent Thunderbird sightings come to us from Missouri and Illinois. Thunderbird reports peaked in the 1940s, but occasional sightings still occur today. The Thunderbird is universally described as large, with a wingspan greatly in excess of 15 feet. The body of the bird is black with a white ring around the neck. The head of the creature is sometimes described as featherless, like that of a vulture, and this trait may be the source of the dinosaurian or reptilian attributes sometimes ascribed to the creature.

This description closely matches that of the California condor, the only difference being that the California condor does not have a white ring around its neck. However, the Andean condor, from South America, does have a white ring around its neck. These similarities have caused many people to speculate that a misidentified condor of one species or another is responsible for Thunderbird sightings. Such a misidentification is, in this author's opinion, unlikely, since Thunderbirds have been described as the "size of a small plane," and the wingspan of the condor is just over 10 feet. It is possible, though, that the Thunderbird is a species of vulture closely related to but entirely distinct from both the Andean and the California condor.

In a strange twist, the Thunderbird has been adopted by Young Earth Creationists as a sort of mascot. Young Earth Creationists are those Christians who, based on their interpretation of the Bible, believe that the Earth is only 6,000 years old. This is contrary to mountains of evidence widely accepted by the scientific community. In order to clear the way for their worldview, these Christians attempt to discredit the scientific community wherever possible. One common way they attempt to do this is to provide evidence of humans coexisting with animals that went extinct before humans came onto the scene. Since some Thunderbird observers report features that may be interpreted as pterosaur-like, Young Earth Creationists are eager to find concrete evidence of its existence. While it is wonderful to have such a dedicated group keeping their eyes to the sky, serious cryptozoologists should be cautious concerning reports coming from Young Earth Creationists, as their zeal may obscure a sober assessment of the facts.

WASHINGTON'S EAGLE

There is no cryptid with a finer, more detailed description than Washington's Eagle. The fact that this description comes from none other than the esteemed John James Audubon adds to the mystery surrounding this bird. Audubon was a naturalist most famous for his paintings of birds, which he released in his seminal work *The Birds of America*, published in 1827. This book contained nearly 500 color plates documenting many of the continent's birds. Original printings of *The Birds of America* are now the most expensive books on the market, having fetched upwards of $11 million at auction. Audubon's work is held in such high regard that the foremost avian conservation society in the United States is named after him, along with dozens of schools, parks, and streets. He is, without a doubt, the most reputable and famous naturalist to have ever documented a cryptid.

While making field observations for his book, Audubon discovered 25 new species of bird. He also was lucky enough to observe and draw the Ivory-Billed Woodpecker, mentioned elsewhere in this publication. But for the cryptozoologist, the most interesting bird in his book must be Washington's Eagle. With a wingspan

Washington's Eagle

of over ten feet, this magnificent bird was by far the largest eagle in North America, indeed the world. Even though Audubon was able to observe, shoot, collect, and paint this creature, many mainstream ornithologists deny that the bird does, or ever did, exist.

Audubon first saw what we now call Washington's Eagle in February of 1814, while aboard a boat on the Upper Mississippi. Audubon believed that this was a new bird, unknown to science, but he was unable to make another observation until a few years later. Eventually, he was able to shoot a specimen and make detailed observations, a summary of which is provided below:

> *Tarsus and toes uniformly scutellate in their whole length. Bill bluish-black, cere yellowish-brown, feet orange-yellow, claws bluish-black. Upper part of the head, hind neck, back, scapulars, rump, tail-coverts, and posterior tibial feathers blackish-brown, glossed with a coppery tint; throat, fore neck, breast, and belly light brownish-yellow, each feather, with a central blackish-brown streak; wing-coverts light grayish-brown, those next the body becoming darker; primary quills dark brown, deeper on their inner webs; secondaries lighter, and on their outer webs of nearly the same light tint as their coverts; tail uniform dark brown.*

Audubon's ornithological peers, perhaps upset at being upstaged by an amateur, dismissed Audubon's claim that he had discovered a new species of eagle. They claimed that Audubon had simply misidentified an immature bald eagle. Audubon, however, was very familiar with the far more common bald eagle in all stages of its development. The description he provides of Washington's Eagle also differs from immature bald eagles in a number of ways. First, Washington's Eagle is much larger than any bald eagle. Second, the coloration of the feathers and the skin around the beak differs from an immature bald eagle. Finally, Audubon describes Washington's Eagle as having uniform scaling on its legs, something which the bald eagle does not have.

I believe it is highly unlikely that Audubon would have mistaken an immature bald eagle for a new species. He was notoriously meticulous in his observations and was experienced in bird identification. It is equally unlikely that he would have risked ruining his reputation and his livelihood by fabricating a fictional species. It is more likely that Audubon saw a once common species of eagle at the tail end of a severe population drop. It is possible that Washington's Eagle now survives with only a very small population.

Sightings have been made across the eastern United States, most notably in New Hampshire and New Jersey. The most recent sighting comes from 2004, just north of Stillwater, Minnesota. An avid birdwatcher and her husband came across an eagle similar in appearance to an immature bald eagle, but much larger in size and slightly different in coloration. They watched the bird preen itself for nearly half an hour while perching on a snowy bough in a tree along the St. Croix River. When they finally approached to attempt a photograph, the bird took flight and flew upriver, out of sight.

Index of Cryptids

References

1. Iverson, J. B., & McCord, W. P. (1997). Redescription of the Arakan forest turtle *Geoemyda depressa* Anderson 1875 (Testudines: Bataguridae). Chelonian Conservation and Biology, 2, 384-389.

2. Fernando, P., Vidya, T. C., Payne, J., Stuewe, M., Davison, G., Alfred, R. J., ... & Melnick, D. J. (2003). DNA analysis indicates that Asian elephants are native to Borneo and are therefore a high priority for conservation. PLoS Biol.

3. Smith, J. L. B. (1940). A living coelacanthid fish from South Africa. Transactions of the Royal Society of South Africa, 28 (1)

4. Von Koenigswald, G. H. R. (1952). *Gigantopithecus blacki* von Koenigswald, a giant fossil hominoid from the Pleistocene of southern China. American Museum of Natural History.

5. Lankester, E. (1902). On *Okapia*, a new Genus of Giraffidæ, from Central Africa. The Transactions of the Zoological Society of London, 16(6)

6. Le, T. B., Le, Q. H., Tran, M. L., et. al. (2010). Comparative morphological and DNA analysis of specimens of giant freshwater soft-shelled turtle in Vietnam related to Hoan Kiem Lake. Vietnam Journal of Biotechnology, 8, 949-954.

7. Meldrum, D. J. (2004). Midfoot flexibility, fossil footprints, and sasquatch steps: New perspectives on the evolution of bipedalism. Journal of Scientific Exploration, 18(1), 65-79.

8. Griffiths, F., & Lynch, C. (2009). Reflections on the Cottingley Fairies: Frances Griffiths in Her Own Words. JMJ Publications.

9. Rines, R. H., Wyckoff, C. W., Edgerton, H. E., & Klein, M. (1976). Search for the Loch Ness Monster. Technology Review, 78(5), 25-35.

10. Thomson, D. M., Brown, N. N., & Clague, A. E. (1992). Routine use of hair root or buccal swab specimens for PCR analysis: advantages over using blood. Clinica Chimica Acta, 207(3)

11. World Health Organization. (2015). Statistical classification of diseases, injuries, and causes of global death.

12. Tullio, L., Piper, J. (1978) Flora and Fauna of the Southeast. Northern Gavidai Publishing.

13. Acoustics Monitoring Program - (Bloop). Pacific Marine Environment Laboratory. National Oceanic and Atmospheric Administration.

14. Moore, J. (1890). Concerning a skeleton of the great fossil beaver, *Castoroides ohioensis*. Cincinnati Society of Natural History.

15. Thorson, T. B., Cowan, C. M., & Watson, D. E. (1973). Body fluid solutes of juveniles and adults of the euryhaline bull shark *Carcharhinus leucas* from freshwater and saline environments. Physiological Zoology, 46(1), 29-42.

16. Hatai, K., & Hoshiai, G. (1992). Mass mortality in cultured coho salmon (*Oncorhynchus kisutch*) due to *Saprolegnia parasitica coker*. Journal of Wildlife Diseases, 28(4), 532-536.

17. Simberloff, D. (2010). RN Reed and GH Rodda (eds): Giant constrictors: biological and management profiles and an establishment risk assessment for nine large species of pythons, anacondas, and the boa constrictor. Biological Invasions, 12(7), 2375-2377.

18. Raynal, Michel, and Jean-Pierre Sylvestre. Cetaceans with two dorsal fins. Aquatic Mammals 17.1 (1991): 31-36.

19. Nuttall, Z. (1895). A Note on Ancient Mexican Folk-Lore. The Journal of American Folklore, 8(29), 117-129.

20. Bargo, M. S. (2001). The ground sloth *Megatherium americanum*: skull shape, bite forces, and diet. Acta Palaeontologica Polonica, 46(2).

21. Kearney, L. S. (1928). The Hodag and Other Tales of the Logging Camps. Democrat Printing Company.

22. Lin, Y. L., Borenstein, L. A., Selvakumar, R., Ahmed, R., & Wettstein, F. O. (1992). Effective vaccination against papilloma development by immunization with L1 or L2 structural protein of cottontail rabbit papillomavirus. Virology, 187(2), 612-619.

23. Emory, K. P. (1959). Origin of the Hawaiians. The Journal of the Polynesian Society, 68(1), 29-35.

24. Pihlström, H. (2011). Tetrapod zoology book one. Historical Biology, 23(4), 439-440.

25. Dundas, R. G. (1999). Quaternary records of the dire wolf, *Canis dirus*, in North and South America. Boreas, 28(3), 375-385.

26. Cornelius, J.P., & Shakey, I.M. (2002). Long Island as North American wildlife disease epicenter. Journal of American Zoopathology, 18, 260-289.

27. McCain, E. B., & Childs, J. L. (2008). Evidence of resident jaguars (*Panthera onca*) in the southwestern United States and the implications for conservation. Journal of Mammalogy, 89(1), 1-10.

28. Watts, A. B., Spence, D. W., Holzenburg, A. K., Toler, D. G., Prychitko, T. M., Zhang, F., ... & Smith, R. (2012). Novel North American Hominids, Next Generation Sequencing of Three Whole Genomes and Associated Studies Melba S. Ketchum (Corresponding author) Patrick W. Wojtkiewicz 2.

29. Dougal, G.C., Mirela, P.L., & Knut, Y. I. (1998) Periodic emergences of the Texarkana Mud Dragon. South Central Entomological Journal. 21(5), 36-55.

30. Suárez, W. I., & Olson, S. L. (2014). Systematics and distribution of the giant fossil barn owls of the West Indies (Aves: Strigiformes: Tytonidae). Zootaxa, 4020(3), 533-553.

31. Fitzpatrick, J. W., Lammertink, M., Luneau, M. D., Gallagher, T. W., Harrison, B. R., Sparling, G. M., ... & Swarthout, S. B. (2005). Ivory-billed Woodpecker (*Campephilus principalis*) persists in continental North America. Science, 308(5727), 1460-1462.

32. Allen, J. A. (1870). What is the "Washington Eagle?". The American Naturalist, 4(9), 524-527.

Dr. Courtney A. Shepherd lives and teaches in Billings, Montana. When not in the classroom, Courtney can be found exploring the beautiful and rugged American West with Biscuit, the world's greatest dog.

Zach Taylor lives and works in Minneapolis, Minnesota. Zach's contributions to this publication include drawings of the Altamaha-ha, the Chupacabra, the Thunderbird, the Sasquatch, the Dogman, the Lone Pine Mountain Devil, the Loveland Frog, and the Ozark Howler.